FRESH
FOOTPRINTS
IN SEARCH OF A LOST GOD

JOHN HOUGHTON

malcolm down
PUBLISHING

21 20 19 18 17   7 6 5 4 3 2 1

First published in 2017 by Malcolm Down Publishing Ltd
www.malcolmdown.co.uk

British Library Cataloguing in Publication Data
A catalogue record for this book is available from the British Library.

ISBN 978-1-910786-78-9

Cover design by Esther Kotecha
Art direction by Sarah Grace
Printed in the UK

To my wife, Jan,
and to
Debbie and James, Sharon and Matthew, Steve and Emma,
my personal heroes of faith.
With love and honour.

Acknowledgements

I am grateful to many people over many years who have helped shape this book, and in recent times those who have patiently listened to and debated its contents. In particular, I wish to thank Henry Morse, Mike Carter, Mark Warner, Andrew Whitman and the members of Wessex Writers who read and critiqued all or parts of the various drafts that led to the final manuscript. Special thanks to Ros Tatton-Bennett for proofreading the whole, and to my wife and muse, Jan, for her unfailing encouragement, advice and patient listening. The resultant work is my own responsibility. I have sought to quote others responsibly and intend no malice, personal judgement, defamation or distortion on those rare occasions where we might differ.

Contents

Life

1. Starting Out

Our society said, 'Abracadabra', and God disappeared! Was it a conjuring trick, a clever illusion, or did God truly vanish from our lives? If so, where has he hidden?

I became a God-searcher just in time for the closing down sale of his chain of shops. Churches went under the hammer, vicars no longer believed their own faith, and God was pronounced dead. But I possessed an insatiable curiosity and I wanted to find out for myself. So I began looking.

My own journey is a personal one, but by no means unique. I would expect it to be the same for you should you undertake it. It is not for me to tell you what to believe; you must find that out for yourself. All truth claims are refracted through our own cultural spectacles, but that doesn't mean we can never agree on what we see. As an artist, I have good colour perception but one of my children is partly colour blind, yet we both agree on what we are seeing. It is just nuanced by our perceptions. A door is a door, whatever its colour.

My journey led me to discover God for myself – though both the nature of that journey and its outcome proved stranger than ever I could have imagined. Even if you reach a different conclusion, I hope you will come to understand better what it really means to be a God-follower, rather than just accepting the popular misconceptions that float around like dead leaves in a winter's puddle. At least you will then be able to speak from knowledge.

A friend of mine once said, 'Why has it taken me forty-three years to discover that the God I didn't believe in was the same one you don't believe in, either! Why has no one ever told me the truth before?' A fair point.

The reason for this book? Based on my own experience and that of many others, I want to invite you on a quest, a treasure hunt to find a lost God. Specifically, the lost God that Christians and others claim to experience in their lives – though that doesn't mean you have to become a Christian. There are plenty living outside of formal religion who are on this journey, as well as those within. To reassure you from the outset, I have no intention of adding to the world's religions with yet another of my own. Nor am I a spiritual scalp-collector. And apart from the price of this book, I don't want your money.

Stranger on the Shore

I love the seaside and I picture this journey as a walk along the seashore. As a metaphor it provides a good model to help us on our personal inner pilgrimage and for tracing some fresh footprints in the well-washed sand. The seashore offers us a unique interface between land and sea, a place that defies simple polarities and over-rigid certainties. Instead, we observe patterns emerging from apparent chaos. Running seas, crashing waves, dangerous rip tides, and millpond stillness interweave with sandy, pebbly, shifting beaches and craggy cliffs, enticing coves and ever-changing skies.

Nothing is ever still for long, yet everything is as changeless as the tides and the seasons. The shoreline is a wild and beautiful place!

It is also a place where we encounter many examples of a wave-form pattern that will prove foundational to our understanding of the universe, our own psyches, and the possible nature of God. More of that later.

Learning to 'think shore' is one of the secrets of wisdom, for wisdom is more at home with both/and than with either/or. For example much of shore life is adapted to be comfortable both in water and on dry land. Think for a moment of crabs, turtles, sea lions, wading birds, to name but a few. Many of our personal and social ills boil down to making everything either/or when life doesn't always work like that. Let me begin with a question. What are human beings, and how should we treat one another? Classic Christian theology says we are all made in the image of God and therefore of infinite worth. How humane we are in our behaviour may vary, but there is no question about how human we are.

Or is there? History sadly tells a different story. We have treated blacks and Indians as subhuman, declared some humans 'the enemy' to be destroyed like vermin. We have reduced others to cruel servitude, granted women and children less than human status. We have persecuted gays, foreigners, so-called lower classes. In short, our 'us and them' mentality drives 'them' out to sea while we stay safe in our fortresses on dry land. This is what we will call binary or dualistic thinking, and it lies at the root of so many of our problems.

The sea shore may not be a perfect metaphor but its both/and character invites us to look at life differently. Thinking shore enlarges our minds and understanding way beyond simple yes/no, winners and losers, black or white categories. My hope is that this will be a journey of discovery, an opportunity not simply to learn some facts, but to explore a different way of thinking.

For the moment, right from the start let's just focus on what kind of seeker you might be. Clearly, I don't know you personally but I'll assume that you have some curiosity about life, and some dissatisfaction with how things are, otherwise you wouldn't be reading this book. Yet your search will be uniquely your own because our journeys towards or away from God are always personal ones. They are also seldom well planned – more like a series of accidents than calculated ventures. Emotion influences our direction probably more than intellect.

In my own case, a hotchpotch of apparently random events over a long period of time somehow coalesced into the possibility that God existed and that he might even be knowable. The full story can wait, but coming from a non-religious, non-church, working-class background in North London hardly predisposed me to start out on any meaningful quest.

I did have questions, however. Like, as a five-year-old, why did I dream that I journeyed the cosmos to discover that it was a colossal ellipse ending behind the dustbins in our back yard? What was the thirty-foot-high series of multicoloured gothic arches that appeared outside the window during a storm in that same year? Who was the old man who appeared from nowhere and pointed to where I would find my lost shoe at the bottom of the churned up pond into which I had fallen, and who then disappeared before me and my mates in broad daylight? Why did the dum-ti-dum bell of a little Anglican church always say, 'Come to church' in my head? I never did. Worse still, what was the voice that spoke in my mind from a large ash tree in Spaniards Wood, Hampstead, telling me what my destiny was? I was only nine, for goodness' sake!

In spite of a relentlessly scientific and rationalistic education, something nagged inside me. Were these, and other experiences like them, epiphanies, close encounters of a spiritual kind? Could there be more to life? Science can only observe and measure, but how could you measure the unmeasurable? The artistic, creative side of my personality demanded answers that science can never supply.

Why the Interest?

So, why your particular interest?

Maybe you were raised in a religious environment, possibly even a Christian one. You perhaps performed all the prescribed rituals to the best of your ability, tried to be a good person and sometimes, in spite of valid doubts, tried to believe that it's all true. But it has not satisfied your deepest spiritual longings. Disappointed, even despairing, you concluded that it doesn't work for you – but deep down maybe you wish it had. Another look, perhaps?

You may have suffered at the hands of religion. People you trusted and respected may turn out to be hypocrites. Sadly, it is possible to be Christian in belief without being Christlike in behaviour. You might have been personally slighted by a broken relationship. Perhaps you have been abused sexually or otherwise. Maybe you felt brainwashed by the dogma and by dominant leaders, even threatened with eternal punishment if you raised questions or failed to conform to the expected norm. People often feel confused by such experiences. Their pain leaves them with all sorts of unanswered questions. If that's you, I hope this exploration might assist your healing.

Many have felt social outcasts because their legs were too long, their skirts too short and their tops too low. Oh, and their music too loud and too broad; their reading matter, too. Your sexuality may be uncertain, your manners uncouth. Mrs Tut-Tut and Mr O'Dear have driven many from their churches and religious establishments with scarcely needing to say a word to your face. You just know you don't fit.

If you have an enquiring mind, it may be that you never had honest answers to honest questions. In some quarters even asking questions is frowned upon; you should just believe. But your questions are valid. Can God still have a place in a world ruled by science and technology? How can there be a God of love given so much appalling suffering in this world? Does everything have to be taken as literally true in the Bible? Hasn't evolution disproved the existence of God, anyway? You might call yourself an agnostic or an atheist, but you still possess an open mind to explore what others believe. Curiosity alone is a good enough reason to join the trip.

Then again, you might be carrying guilty secrets in your life and you are just terrified of being found out. Perhaps you pleaded with God to deal with your difficult habit, to set you free; but in your case he hasn't. So you feel unworthy, unwanted, maybe angry at God – if he exists. You may feel that God hates you. Your loved friend or relative is sick, and it's all your fault because of something you must have done to offend God – perhaps even 'the unforgivable sin'.

Or, maybe you have simply lost your bearings. Difficult circumstances, overwhelming pressure, traumatic bereavement, unanswered prayer – all these things and more may have crushed your spirit as you struggled to survive. You have come through the worst but emotionally you are shot through, physically you are washed out, and you have lost contact with God. You regret that happening but it has still left a gap in your life that needs filling.

On a more positive note, your personal history may include half-spoken experiences that hint at something more to life – a greater power maybe, a guardian angel, a deeply moving epiphany that could point to one of those close encounters of the spiritual kind. A dream that stays with you. An uncanny feeling that sends tingles down your spine but attracts you, nonetheless. Is there another dimension to life, another story to the one our culture tells us? You want to take a look.

This is an itch that needs to be scratched. Our consumer society has failed to meet our deeper needs. Large and growing numbers of people are looking to older wisdom in a contemporary context, hoping for a transcendence that can give our lives a meaning beyond simply acquisition and survival. Some define themselves as New Age, Pagan or Wiccan; others simply hunger for a more meaningful and integrated life.

So, whether you are religious or non-religious by temperament or experience, join me down at the waterfront, and walk for a while on this shore of infinite possibilities. It may just include finding that lost God and the true meaning of life. Welcome to the trail!

2. How God Got Lost

Since this book is about finding a lost God, we should begin by asking ourselves how God managed to get lost in the first place!

This is largely a problem for those of us, mostly white, who have grown up in the West. The majority of people in the world believe in God in some form or other. They acknowledge the reality of a spiritual life and it profoundly shapes how they live, be they Hindus, Jews, Muslims, Buddhists, Christians – Anglican, Free church, Roman Catholic, Russian or Greek Orthodox, whatever. These numbers probably account for around 85 per cent of the world's population. Faith, of some kind, is alive and well in the contemporary world.

But not in the West.

Some claim that God died in the trenches of World War I; others that it was in the concentration camps of World War II. Well, maybe, but in spite of those dreadful atrocities there was a significant revival of popular Christianity during the aftermath of the Second World War. Much of that has continued into our present day, and many churches still thrive and make a considerable contribution to the well-being of society.

Others have claimed that the rise of modern science made God unnecessary and irrelevant, but the majority of those great scientific discoveries were made by devout believers who found that their faith inspired their researches rather than deterred them. As I hope we will come to see, science need be no enemy of faith, nor faith the enemy of science.

Perhaps it was not suffering but luxury that made us lose God. There is little doubt that modern technological advances have brought huge benefits to Western life. I, for one, do not wish to deny those benefits. There is a cost to modernity, though. It has led to a loss of meaning and a lack of soul satisfaction. Our frenetic consumer-driven world of instant gratification rings hollow to anyone who really wants to know what life is about. Wealth increases neurosis, not happiness. Glut creates gluttons, not grace.

This is why there is a growing search for a more spiritual way of life. You are certainly not alone on this trail. It may have been the road less-travelled but the numbers taking it increase daily.

My personal conviction is that God was lost by the churches themselves. That may sound shocking but I think it is true.

Dud Deism

As we begin our journey, leaving behind for the moment the battle-scarred beaches, the oceanographic research labs and the pleasure palaces on the pier, we soon come across the skeletal remains of an old sailing ship. Look closely and you will still find its faded name on a piece of rotting wood. It was called, *The Deist*. It was launched in the seventeenth century to convey a cargo of ideas that we should briefly consider.

Deism is the name given to a belief in a supreme being or creator, a higher power that does not intervene in the universe. He does not speak, appear, direct our lives, do miracles or answer prayer. This is a God who wound up the cosmic clock and was so exhausted by the effort that he went into permanent retirement! He is unknown and unknowable.

Such a being was as good as useless. God in the abstract, left people cold and mystified. Imagine a baker no longer believing in bread, yet trying to sell you the idea of 'bread-ness' but with no tangible bread on the shelves. You would turn elsewhere for food – and that's just what millions did.

The churches that embraced this notion of God must shoulder much of the blame for losing him. Many opted instead for sterile formality and respectable middle-class cleverness. Faith was downgraded to the polite hypocrisy that occurs when God is removed to a place far beyond our reach – the mask of religion hiding the unreality beneath. As Fr Richard Rohr observes, 'The right language is very often the best disguise for the wrong identity.'[1] The ship has long since sunk but like the famed *Marie Celeste*, the spectre remains and still haunts our minds. We retain the ghost image of a supreme being, probably male and monarchical, unmoved by our plight, untouched by our pain or our prayers, unknowable and no longer relevant.

Although this distant Deist God has disappeared from our world, as well he might, and good luck to him, sometimes it's hard to shake off the image of this old hulk. In the absence of anything better it's the only one we retain. It is also the unthinking default setting of our popular media.

Our first step must be to leave the old wreck behind; this is not what we are seeking! God is not the old man in the sky that you can only hope to see through the Hubble Space Telescope. Even if that were possible, and although you possessed a doctorate in astrophysics, that observation would in any case remain little more than a piece of debatable and sterile logic. It would make absolutely no difference to your life or mine.

Many people came to this conclusion in the 1960s. An austere God whose only purpose, if any, was to send most of us to hell at the end of time, may have suited a militaristic, authoritarian and hierarchical society, but, as Bob Dylan put it back then, 'The times, they are a-changin'.' Up ahead we see a beach party – cool music, trendy fashion and free sex, liberally marinated in a haze of drugs and alcohol. A cultural and religious revolution declared the old God dead along with his repressive views on sex and his liking for violence. Flower power was born under the shadow of the Bomb.

Love versus napalm. Romanticism versus rationalism. Tune in; chill out. Have fun. Millions of us did just that.

By the end of the twentieth century, as the pendulum swung to and fro, few people knew what to believe any longer. There was no big story, no certainty, no meaning. An agnostic and highly individualistic post-modern society concluded that your truth is right for you; my truth is right for me.

Postmodernism possessed the merit of tolerance. It was allowable, for a short space in time, to talk about your faith in God – or no faith – and you could be treated with respect. Dialogue was possible. But postmodernism also created a vacuum. The stage was set for the rise of the censorious and strident right-wing and left-wing fundamentalism that we see today. The party has given way to barbed wire and bombs, and everybody is photographing the evidence as ammunition for their own cause.

God hit the global headlines on 11 September 2001. Literally, out of the blue. To be precise, it was the aerial attacks on the New York Twin Towers done in the name of God that made the news.

Suddenly, the West had a new enemy. It had seen off Hitler. It had watched the fall of Soviet Communism. China was now a trading partner. Atheism had lost its political force; it was now little more than a luxury for a privileged intellectual establishment, while religion played its traditional small and benign role in civic life. Overnight, all that changed and religion moved to the top of the agenda. The new enemy was religious. It believed in God, did its acts of terrorism in the name of God, wished to subjugate or destroy all who stood in the way of its God. We were thrown back to the Middle Ages.

Politically, the West declared a global war on terrorism, effectively putting its own people under mass surveillance while hunting down the bomb makers.

Religiously, a new breed of old atheists declared that belief in God was an unhealthy delusion and the cause of all our ills. It's time for us to scale a small cliff and take a look from their perspective. However, if you are happy to accept the existence of God and are totally fazed by science, you may want to skip these next three chapters and read on from chapter 6.

before he realizes that his only hope is not that he can live
forever, but that he can pass on his love and knowledge and
his talents for writing. Can he learn to let go, live and share
with another for the rest of his life?

3. The Case for Atheism

Atheism, the belief that there is no God, has been around for a long time, certainly as far back as Democritus (500 BC) and it is mentioned in the fourteenth Psalm of David (1041 – 971 BC) thus: 'The fool says in his heart, "There is no God."'

The arguments depend on what we mean by the term 'God' and, just as importantly, on why we believe in one. Or don't believe in one. It's likely that David was simply referring to the folly of those who denied God's existence so that they could justify an immoral or criminal life without fearing any consequences. But many modern atheists are highly moral and thoroughly decent people. Atheist doesn't equate necessarily to bad person! It may simply be a neutrally held intellectual position.

That said, there are vocal atheists who express their atheism in strongly emotive and antagonistic terms, and decidedly anti-Christian ones. This often appears to arise from their having abandoned a religious background for reasons that aren't just intellectual but emotional, too. They have gone on the offensive and gained considerable publicity from the intellectual establishment, in some cases even trying to form atheist churches.

If they are simply rejecting the old Deist God and all the stultifying effects of formal religion, I am inclined to side with them because the God they reject is the one I would reject, too! Such an impersonal, Spiritless belief is enough to turn anyone atheist! However, we must recognise a distinct bias in their arguments.

Emotional atheism is not so objective as it might at first sight seem to be. Nor is it necessarily so tough-minded. For instance, all honest human beings wrestle with the problem of human suffering. It's all very well to declare that it's no more than blind chance, bad luck and meaninglessness, but that offers little comfort or even explanation for the sheer quantity and intensity of pain that ravages this planet.

Every time we ask, 'If there's a God, then why the pain and suffering?' we are expressing a wish, a desire that there was a God who would put right all the wrongs and look after us poor souls a sight better than he appears to. In the ironic words of Samuel Beckett's character in *Endgame*: 'God doesn't exist – the bastard!' Or in the plaintive words of Julian Barnes: 'I don't believe in God, but I miss him.'[2] Perhaps deep down we still wish for a God who intervenes, someone who will listen and who will answer our prayers.

Has Science Disproved God?

However, today's emotional 'new atheist' appeal is mostly to the sciences and a highly questionable claim that science has disproved God's existence. It takes only a moment to realise that this is a nonsensical statement because the role of science is simply to observe, measure, repeat, and apply its findings through technology. Wonderful as science is, it doesn't possess the tools to measure the immeasurable, and what can't be measured is beyond the province of science to tackle, just as are many other things, like love or beauty or goodness. You can measure sex and even the psycho-physical responses of people in love, but you cannot measure the reality that the human race calls love – as any person who is actually in love will tell you.

The statement, 'Science has disproved the existence of God,' is also logically absurd. It assumes that we know everything there is to know, which plainly we don't. Imagine a sphere containing all existing and all possible human knowledge. How much does even the brainiest know? As Isaac Newton put it, 'To myself I am only a child playing on the beach, while vast oceans of truth lie undiscovered before me.' The seashore teaches you humility, if nothing else.

After a lifetime of study, education and experience, I have concluded that I know almost nothing about almost everything, and that is pretty well true of everyone else. It is then perfectly reasonable that God might exist in a dimension we have yet to discover. The great scientist Werner Heisenberg said, 'The first gulp from the glass of natural sciences will turn you into an atheist, but at the bottom of the glass God is waiting for you.' Maybe we just need to drink deeper.

Much of modern science is based on reductionism. The word means precisely that; we deconstruct and reduce everything to its smallest component parts and hope thereby to understand the origin and function of what it is we are analysing. For example, given a motor car, we have the ability to take it to pieces. We can work out its mechanics, if necessary right down to its atoms and molecules, and then put it together again, and even to modify it. This is what we do with genetic engineering.

Reductionism has proved to be an immensely powerful and impressive tool in our quest for knowledge and understanding of the natural world. So much so that many believe it is the one tool needed to fully comprehend the universe. This reductionism is then viewed as the only true and reliable knowledge. So when people say, 'Prove God exists', they often mean, prove it by this method.

But suppose God is not an entity or being that can be proved by this method? Many have pointed out the limits and even dangers of scientific reductionism. Can everything be solved by reducing it to mathematical equations? Can human realities like love, beauty or goodness really be reduced to a formula? Can you seduce someone from a textbook? Even more, cause them to love you freely? The older response was to declare that because these qualities cannot be measured they do not exist. God is often treated this way.

This hard-nosed approach was tried on a grand scale in the twentieth century by the Russian and Chinese Communists, and by the Nazis. Under these regimes, society could now be systematically engineered, personalities analysed and manipulated, dissidents brainwashed or disposed of as no more than faulty electrochemical machines. These 'assured results of modern science' crushed the souls of millions in the incinerators of war, concentration camps and soviet gulags.

Militant atheists often like to blame all wars and oppression on religion. Certainly, religion has caused its fair share over the centuries and even though this must be qualified by the fact that ruthless rulers have used religion as a lever rather than religion being the cause, it is nonetheless reprehensible. However, all these wars pale into insignificance compared to the sheer scale of numbers and brutality of the wars and violence instigated by political atheism. It might be better to recognise this simple reality.

Looking back, the process of deconstruction, of reductionism, appears crude, not to say, ludicrous, when applied to society and human personality. This is to say nothing about qualities such as beauty, truth and goodness which were so easily discarded, along with the possibility of God. Arthur Koestler dubbed it 'nothing-but-ism'.[3] Thankfully, we are moving on to more holistic and dynamic models of reality in which we recognise that higher levels of complexity like human personality do not lend themselves to simple reductionist tools. No sane person wants a return to Stalin's gulags or Hitler's concentration camps.

As a lover of science, I have a deep respect for scientific progress, but I am also aware of the limits to which we can apply scientific methodology. For example, to do so we must assume that everything can be reduced to mathematics. But that assumes the existence of measurable time and space. What about if we transcend time and space? Mathematics and theoretical physics fail us at this point simply because there is nothing to measure.

Let me give you an example. My wife and I were once on holiday in the south-west of France and our campsite led down to a west-facing cliff-top seascape. One clear evening we wandered down to watch the sunset. Many others had done the same, and there were people from a variety of European countries present. It was one of those perfect sunsets and we were able to watch the orange ball sink to the horizon with not a trace of haze or cloud. As the very last fraction of the sun disappeared beyond the sea, with no prompting, the entire crowd emitted a collective, 'Ah!' It was a very human moment and a quite profound one.

Now, almost everybody present would have known that the sunset was just the result of our planet revolving eastwards until our location was no longer tangential to the sun. Everybody knew that tomorrow the sun would rise in the east. From a scientific perspective, the 'Ah!' was unnecessary. Emotionally, it was a corporate response to beauty, tinged with awe and wonder, and that cannot be measured; it can only be experienced or imagined.

Over-apply scientific reductionism and we may lose the very thing we are trying to measure. Dismantle a rose and you no longer have 'a thing of beauty is a joy for ever'.[4] Over-analyse your perception of beauty and you may lose that perception and diminish yourself in the process. Worse, you may start calling it an illusion because you can no longer sense it yourself. It's a bit like losing your sense of smell because you smoke or have sinus problems. Because you can't smell the rose you believe that it has no scent. This self-imposed limitation is why some atheists talk about the God delusion. I can't see what you claim to see, they say, so you must be deluded! Not exactly the high point of science, logic or common sense!

The plain fact is that modern science is not as objective or assured as we would like it to be as a basis for proof and truth. Personal reputations, military demands, university funding, philosophic trends, fashion, politics, even climate, all have a bearing on what is accepted as scientific orthodoxy. Many claims of fact are little more than mathematical equations based on selective data and personal preconceptions. That is why truly intelligent scientists prefer to talk about degrees of probability rather than absolute proof. For example, combine hydrogen and oxygen and there is a high probability that you will get water, H2O. That's easy. It's a lot harder when it comes to the origins of the universe, and the probability of any current theory being true is very much lower.

Now this next bit may be a bit of a scrabble if you lack a background in science. The exotic world of quantum physics further compounds our problem of reality and it challenges us at the level of our deepest held modern beliefs, our paradigms. Ever since the ancient Greek philosopher, Aristotle (384 BC), produced a hierarchy that put *substantia* or 'stuff' at the top of the reality tree, we in the West have majored on materialism right down to our present day consumerism. But quantum physics appears to reverse that priority and gives it instead to relationship.

In quantum states it seems that the experimenter has a profound effect on the experiment even if he tries not to. Similarly, there is the phenomenon of quantum entanglement, which suggests that once an atom has interacted with another, even though they fly off to opposite ends of the universe, they will continue to influence each other's behaviour because of their first encounter. That is truly mind-boggling if you are a materialist reductionist. But not if your paradigm makes relationship the priority. This thought alone could change your entire world view.

Science is never complete so it cannot by definition ever speak in final absolutes. Nor is it by any means the only tool in the box of human enquiry. 'Scientific' atheism then cannot be considered an advance; it is only an unproven and unprovable opinion.

4. Creation and Evolution

Having scrambled up this particular cliff, we should at least enjoy the view. It's a clear night and the stars are brilliant. Maybe you know some of the constellations. I can usually manage the Plough and Orion, and often the Pleiades. I'll find Venus and Mars, too, but I live in a built-up area so it's not so easy.

People have always studied the night heavens and in less polluted times they could see countless more stars than most of us today. Ancient peoples saw them relationally and some brilliant but unknown artist one day drew the constellations that we still recognise as the Zodiac. People began to call these patterns gods; and yet others began to tell fortunes based on their movements. For the record, the Genesis creation story rejects all that by simply stating of God, 'He also made the stars.'

Well, did he, or didn't he?

The debate over creation and evolution has raged for almost 150 years now. It is today still heated, and in some countries political. It is also not very important. That will sound surprising, but let me give you some reasons for saying this.

I believe the debate between creationists and evolutionists is largely a waste of time because it plays into the hands of the old Deist notion of God; somebody so old, so distanced, and only really needed as a prime cause to get the whole show on the road. Christians, particularly, are wrong-footing themselves from the start.

There is no need to delve into detailed arguments about creation versus evolution. The Genesis story provides an ageless story of creation that answers children's usual 'why - how - where - who - what?' questions. 'Why does it get light and dark?' 'Where do animals come from?' 'Why do we wear clothes?' 'Why don't we worship stars?' 'What is an elephant?' Put the answers into a format of seven days and nights and we have an easily memorable, non-scientific (though not necessarily unscientific) explanation of our earthly environment that can be grasped by almost anyone. It simply claims that God is behind it all and that creation is good.

Our current scientific orthodoxy is that the universe began with a big bang (well, big is a meaningless term when there was nothing else to compare it with, and the bang was silent because there was no medium through which to transmit sound and nobody to hear it!), and that life evolved through natural selection. The idea needs qualifying. First, none of this is as proven or as likely as popular scientists pretend. Many unanswered questions remain along with an embarrassing lack of evidence at key points in the theories. To take just one example, there is no real evidence of one species changing into another. The missing links, the transitional species, are still missing. That necessitated the idea of punctuated equilibrium, sudden, unexplained leaps from one species to another. But it's not proven.

Secondly, we still hit the limits of scientific knowledge when we propose an initial event to start the ball rolling. It has nothing to do with how long ago it may have occurred but with the fact that however far back we go in measurable time, however many other universes we may speculate exist, we cannot reach before the beginning. Science is about measuring time and space and making connections, but before the beginning there was no time and no space, only nothing, or something that cannot be measured, something that is by definition beyond science.

This is why it is impossible to prove or to disprove the existence of God by the scientific theory of origins. Let me explain.

An atheist is required to believe that, quite randomly, for no reason whatsoever, and with no energy source, a wondrous particle appeared out of nothing and nowhere. This particle had the power to replicate itself from more nothingness, and to differentiate itself with no pre-existing plan, and with no other energy source, until it became enough stuff to cause a large explosion that gave us the universe that we now know. We can debate the subsequent mechanisms all we like but we are still stuck with a *non sequitur* at the beginning: something came out of absolute nothingness and that something was exotic enough to make more of itself out of nothingness. Given all we know, that takes some believing, and it's dishonest to resort to special pleading for this one instance. Yet based on probability theory it is argued that there must have occurred one chance in infinity – this initial blip. That's as bad as bringing in an angel to make your sums work!

It is only a little easier for the God-believer. He or she starts not with nothingness but with eternal nonmaterial Presence. An I AM. The fundamental of the universe is not a void but a living Personality, a Mind with intelligence and life. This is the Logos, or primary Source, that initiated the cosmos, creating and accommodating himself to time and space. In English we call him God the Creator. Something comes from Someone. Once again we may debate the subsequent processes but at least we have a cause, and that fits with our known perceptions of the universe. Is it proof? No, it takes some believing because it, too, is beyond the reach of science.

A belief in God's existence does have one advantage over atheism and that is common sense. We live in a contingent, that is, a cause and effect universe. Even chaos and randomness seem bent on producing patterns that are the result of one thing leading to another. Go back as far as our current scientific theory allows and we are still faced with the question, 'Why anything, even nothing?' and that includes why the most simple fundamental forces. Why even chaos? Why a starting point?

The moment there is stuff there is time and space. Your

coffee mug exists in 2017 and has a space in the cupboard. Stuff has to have an origin, because all stuff is cause and effect; it is contingent. Your coffee cup was manufactured. By definition, the very first stuff, the original particle, must start time and space, which means that the first particle must originate from a source before time and space.

Given where this logic might take us, some have argued for the existence of other parallel universes as the origin of ours. Naturally, we could never connect with such universes, so to suggest them is simply to mark the dead end of scientific exploration. Push the question back into the unknown and you have solved nothing except make it older!

For me at least it makes more sense to acknowledge the existence of a Source and to agree with the Bible when it states, 'By faith we understand that the universe was formed at God's command, so that what is seen was not made out of what was visible' (Hebrews 11:3). You must, naturally, choose your own faith, but recognise that for neither theism or atheism can you claim scientific proof for something that is by definition beyond the reach of science.

What also helps me believe in the existence of a good God is the fact that we live in the most amazing convenience store imaginable, an Aladdin's cave of resources that goes far beyond our simple need for survival or the biological connection between our environment and our evolution. Let me give you a simple example of what I mean.

We've always wanted to fly like the birds and eventually we worked out how they do it. We made our first aeroplanes from wood and canvas, but they couldn't carry many people. Within a short while we uncovered abundant deposits of a strong lightweight element called aluminium that allowed us to build better aeroplanes. We wanted to go faster so we invented the jet engine, but aluminium couldn't take the heat, so we conveniently found another lightweight, strong element called titanium that could. Then we wanted to give our plane windows. Well, we can make glass from sand, but because of another 'convenience' we could use the same stuff to make silicon chips and steer our craft by computer.

This is just one example of the millions of things we can do using the raw materials of this planet; and they are all here, the entire set of elements exists here. This is a good planet for humankind, a place where our inventiveness is matched by all the resources we need. It might even have been designed for us! Indeed, it isn't beyond the bounds of credibility that a loving deity would provide all that was needed for those made in his image to fulfil their divine destiny, which is to nurture and develop the planet's resources for the common good. For me, at least, it's too good not to be true. Frankly, atheism requires that we are too lucky by half because however old we think the universe to be and however large, the laws of probability just don't allow for the complexity and convenience of our existence.

The truth is it takes a leap of faith to be an atheist, and it takes a leap of faith to believe in a Creator. You either believe that nothing made something or you believe that Someone made something. You either believe that the entire process is meaningless, pointless, purposeless, and no more than a mechanical instinct to survive without reason. Or you believe that the universe has meaning and purpose beyond mere existence.

Naturally, it's perfectly all right to believe in a literal seven-day creation as well if you wish, provided that you recognise that it is an article of faith and not a settled scientific proof. The same goes for Darwin's theory of natural selection. It is a belief upon which you can build a limited case, but it is not rock solid science. The ultimate origin of everything relies on massive speculation. Nothing is repeatable in any way that says this is how it must have happened, so nothing is scientifically proven in the manner that, say, sodium and chlorine combine to form common table salt.

However many billions of years ago we propose the event, and however random we make the first spontaneous flicker in the void, however many unreachable parallel universes we suggest, we are reaching an end to knowledge. We might discover more galaxies, but qualitatively it's all more of the same. People on other planets? Maybe, but, interesting as it might be, it offers nothing to get us before the beginning. And, as we have already mentioned, it still leaves God as above and beyond the limits of reductionist science.

5. Before the Beginning

Now, here is a piece of pure speculation on my part. I include it to illustrate the difficulties that both atheists and creationists have when we try to reach beyond the possible frontiers of scientific exploration. But, just supposing we attempted such an explanation of God's origins. It might go something like this . . .

Let's imagine God self-originated.

After all, surely the greatest act of creation, the most godlike of possibilities, would be to create oneself!

Just supposing, before the beginning – and that is so important to remember – once upon a no-time, in a no-place, there was nothing. But then there was something. An infinitesimal dot; a blip in the infinity of nothingness. The only fully free and unbounded event that ever could or would occur. An oscillation, a wave form, a pulse in the void, an eternal and infinite echo that rose and died, and rose and died, and rose and died, and rose again . . . An event, self-energising without limitation, growing in amplitude and multiplying unhindered in frequency until in no time at all, for of course there was no time, it filled the nothingness. Reverberating to an unbounded infinity, evolving, harmonising, integrating until, defined by its own wave form, it differentiated into the reflective fullness of triform Personality – Father, Son and Holy Spirit. God the eternal, infinite Community in Unity. As the old creeds have it: One God, the Son proceeding from the Father, and the Spirit proceeding from the Father and the Son.

How long did this take? Well, no time at all, for there was no time. Need I remind you? How big did he grow? To infinity for there were no dimensions and no limits. Language fails us at this point, and it is way beyond the reach of science, for science can only go back as far as what can be measured, and there was neither light nor darkness, nor time nor space to measure. Pure Personality has no need of either, any more than you or me. God may dwell in unapproachable light or thick darkness with equal ease – immortal, invisible, all-knowing, the only one there before there was a there to be, or a here. Which is why perhaps God designates himself simply as I AM, because that is the absolute plain truth.

After that, of course, everything is easy. God can create a beginning; matter, time and space, the fundamental forces – everything needed to produce the cosmos as we know it. These are the proper realms for science to explore, understand and use for the good of the human race. Intelligently understood, they are the works of God, the brilliant laws of God, for which we thinking beings should give thanks. After all without them we don't even exist.

And since we consider evolution to have produced humans as its highest achievement to date then surely that blip before anything must have evolved instantly into full Personality, otherwise we could not have reached the stage of reflective personality ourselves. That is not to say we are, as we are, the highest stage of evolution, for the Bible certainly speaks of something better still to come. But more of that later.

This version of the uncaused cause is based on faith. How could it be otherwise since it is by definition beyond the reach of science? But it is just as much an act of faith on the part of the atheist to deny it, and for precisely the same reason.

Enough of my speculation. The question, 'God, who invented you?' was put to the former Archbishop of Canterbury, Rowan Williams, by a little girl named Lulu. This is his response.

Dear Lulu,

Your dad has sent on your letter and asked if I have any answers. It's a difficult one! But I think God might reply a bit like this –

'Dear Lulu – Nobody invented me – but lots of people discovered me and were quite surprised. They discovered me when they looked round at the world and thought it was really beautiful or really mysterious and wondered where it came from. They discovered me when they were very, very quiet on their own and felt a sort of peace and love they hadn't expected. Then they invented ideas about me – some of them sensible and some of them not very sensible. From time to time I sent them some hints – specially in the life of Jesus – to help them get closer to what I'm really like. But there was nothing and nobody around before me to invent me. Rather like somebody who writes a story in a book, I started making up the story of the world and eventually invented human beings like you who could ask me awkward questions!'

And then he'd send you lots of love and sign off. I know he doesn't usually write letters, so I have to do the best I can on his behalf. Lots of love from me too.

Archbishop Rowan[5]

That delightful and very human response may be the best any of us can do given our finite minds and limited experiences.

The clue is in the words, 'They discovered me . . .' That is my hope: that our exploration will prove successful.

Many people become bogged down over this issue of science versus religion and it acts for them as an impasse to any further progress. We have to get beyond this either/or argument into something more productive. After all, what help is it to me when I'm struggling with life to be told that my distant origins are totally random? On the other hand, what help is it for me to be told that my faith stands or falls on whether or not I believe in a recent literal seven day creation? The 'random origins theory' is just a piece of questionable maths, and the Genesis story is open to several other legitimate interpretations that really are important to understand without being obsessed with the 'how long ago' question.

A more holistic approach combines science and technology with good theology and in the process reveals a much fuller view of life. This is neatly put by the psalmist: 'The works of the LORD are great, studied by all who have pleasure in them' (Psalm 111:2 NKJV).

Not When But Why

We might then ask ourselves at this point why God should create in the first place. This is a far more significant question than the one that asks when it took place. It is more important to know what something is for than to know how old it is. One of the problems in studying origins is that we become blasé about gigantic numbers. Currently the age of the universe is put at 13.82 billion years. But what does that number really signify? It is incomprehensible the moment we try to give it any meaning. The age of the earth is put at 4.5 billion years, plus or minus half a billion! Frankly, everything could have come and gone, whole civilisations and species leaving no trace of their existence, in a mere million years and we would still be none the wiser.

Currently humans are estimated to have existed for 200,000 years. I have no idea how accurate these figures really are because they are based on a lot of speculation. My point is that in real terms they are meaningless, and offer us nothing of real value for life in the twenty-first century – a century that most Millennial children will not even see through to the end, given how relatively short are our human lives.

History is of little help. We might just manage a sketchy outline of a few thousand years but even that is beyond our experience simply because most of us will be lucky if we make a hundred. It is sobering to realise that almost everything and almost everyone disappears without a trace. Our history and archaeology is largely that of the rich and powerful, of a few artefacts of durable material. The rest we speculate from scraps, and nothing is proven absolutely beyond maybe 10,000 years at the outside.

So, it doesn't matter how old the universe is or whether we developed in an evolutionary manner. These are interesting enquiries and speculations but they can do nothing for our human condition. We will never prove nor disprove God by this means. We don't find meaning, let alone God, through knowing how old everything is. We certainly shouldn't think that evolution somehow disproves Genesis and therefore the existence of God. We would have to do much better than that.

The Genesis story only really deals with human history within our timeframe, and it has the merit of using numbers that we can at least get our heads round. Whether we believe those numbers to be literal or not is a quite separate question and not particularly relevant to this discussion. As we've noted above, the Genesis story lends itself to more than one theistic interpretation, as any half decent theologian will tell you.

What counts is this intensely human perspective designed to tell us that everything we can see is the work of God and that it was made good. It also informs us that God made us in his image as intelligent creatures, capable of moral choices and able to communicate with him. I'm not too fussed about the timeframe – work it out as best you can – but the fact that love will always want to share, that love is creative, that love is good, is the reason why God the Father, Son and Holy Spirit would express himself in creating a universe, and why he would make creatures like us in his own image.

Now to me, interesting as the process of evolution may be, of far more interest and importance is the divine process that is outworking now and in the future. The past I cannot change; my present and future is where the action is.

Children create for the sheer pleasure of it. They paint pictures of their environment in strange colours and draw people with oddly proportioned bodies. They dance wildly for no apparent reason, put on tea parties for cuddly toys, make mud pies, float twig boats in puddles, press flowers and leaves, produce homemade plays for parents, bash musical instruments made of junk, and in a thousand other ways show that they are human. Pity the poor child who is only given a PlayStation or a smartphone with which to amuse themselves!

This pleasurable human activity is also arguably divine. God, like any competent artist, delights in the diversity of his own creative work. If you have been raised on the old clockwork universe model then you may think that everything boils down merely to sex and survival. If nothing else it might make you a rather miserable so-and-so when you contemplate the cosmos, because this reductionism will blind you to the possibility that God simply enjoyed himself when he made the world. God had fun, extravagant fun in making so many different things, adapting so many ideas to produce the profusion of the created world. Why else produce billions of stars, or even 40,000 varieties of bean?

Even so, pleasure isn't the only factor in creation. As a professional writer, I hope somebody will buy my book so that I can eat. I also hope that I might provoke some fresh thinking that will help people handle their lives a bit better. That is my teleology, my endgame, and it transcends the pleasure of writing, or even the arrival of the published book. Although I have no grand pretensions about changing the world, my modest aim of helping you, the reader, is valid enough for me to carry on typing.

God, on the other hand, is entitled to have the grandest of plans in mind for his creation. In accord with his nature and character, his resources and genius are unlimited. His creative processes, the whole grand experiment, can have a legitimate end, a crowning achievement in mind. Recognise the pattern and you can at once see that it is all going somewhere.

The most radical claim is that there was a creation – a starting point – at all. For a long time scientists believed the cosmos was just there for ever. The Bible story was treated as a myth, not because of its seven days but because it implied a beginning, an Alpha point. Then came Darwin, and Einstein, and the rest as they say, is history. With a beginning, and a likely ending.

So, leaving aside the lunatic fringe and the misusers of science, there should be harmony and co-operation between the disciplines rather than antagonism, and that was broadly the mindset of the pioneer scientists who gave us our modern world. The vast majority saw no contradiction between God's book of words, the Bible, and God's book of works, the environment, and both fed each other. The science versus religion dichotomy is simply outmoded and you should feel perfectly respectable in describing yourself as both a Christian, or at least a theist, and a scientist if you so wish.

Apart from prejudice and sheer bigotry it seems fair to state that the existence of God is a reasonable assumption. It is more likely than not and is favoured by the overwhelming balance of probability. Most people across the world are happy to take that for granted.

The real issue for most of us is not whether God exists but what kind of God might he/she/it/they be. What 'shape' might he have? What sort of personality? Would he have strengths and weaknesses? Vulnerabilities even? Would a better understanding help us know what we could expect, especially when we face adversity and life's big questions? Are there clues for us to follow on our exploratory journey? It's time to leave the giddy heights of cliff-top speculation and return to the beach.

6. The Book of Nature

So, we've made it up and down a piece of cliff that often seems an impassable barrier to further exploration. I hope we've realised that it need not be, that science and God study should complement one another rather than compete, and that whether you embrace the theory of evolution or not makes little difference to your belief in God or otherwise.

Instead, back on a stretch of open beach, let's deal with our own albeit short-lived but significant experiences. Let's see if we can identify patterns.

Working on the assumption that the existence of God is a distinct and even likely probability, and at least a possibility that cannot be ruled out, we can proceed with curiosity to find out what we can about him.

There's just one little breakwater to cross. In classic Christian terms, God is described as Father and Jesus as the Son who came to earth unmistakably as a man, while the Spirit is commonly translated as the masculine he. However, we must not jump to hasty conclusions about this proving Christianity or the Bible to be chauvinist and male dominated. Nor must we assume that our current social structure of gender equality is the only or the right one.

Equally, we should not attach sexual gender distinctions or roles to what we mean by God. The creation account in Genesis declares humans, male and female, both to be in the image of God and thus of equal value and status. It also uses a mothering term to describe the Spirit brooding over the primal seas, as well as numerous other 'feminine' descriptions of God. Although spoken in a negative context, when the Trinity declares of Adam and Eve that 'they have become like us', it presumes an equality of spiritual and moral possibility for both sexes.

Maybe gender with God is just of a higher order than we can comprehend and we waste our time on semantics with our he/she/it labels. Certainly none of this stopped the apostle Paul stating unequivocally that 'there is neither male nor female; for you are all one in Christ Jesus' (Galatians 3:28 NKJV). Whatever the functional differences and however they are worked out in any given society, gender equality in worth and identity is a Judeo-Christian invention. So, in spite of our use of language let's ignore describing God in either stereotypical male or female terms. From now on I will use the generic 'he' for readability, though God probably incorporates both gender characteristics. Incidentally, modern translations of the Bible tend to use inclusive language as that better reflects the original meaning of the terms.

In the classic story structure known as the hero's journey it is customary for the reluctant hero to be gifted with some powerful tools from his mentor. Luke Skywalker is given a light sabre in *Star Wars*; Harry Potter receives an owl and a wand; in *The Lord of the Rings* Frodo has a sword, chain mail and a light. To help us in our quest, which let me say is not a fantasy, I am going to offer us three 'books'. The first of these is the created order, the world around us. The second is the Bible, and the third is our own selves.

Using these books we will look for patterns that point to what God might really be like, and to one common pattern in particular. We begin with the book available to all of us.

The Universal Book
Finding God is not like trying to find a Higgs-Boson particle and does not require a Large Hadron Collider and £7 billion in spare change. Clues to what God is like are scattered all around us once you accept the basic reasonable idea that he might exist. Rather

than looking for the proverbial needle in a haystack we simply have to look at the haystack and ask a few questions, like: who built it, and for what purpose, and with what materials, and why this shape?

The created world may not ultimately prove the existence of God but it does tell us what God is like if he does exist. The entire haystack turns out to be a revelation of his beauty and genius. In the words of an ancient songwriter: 'The heavens broadcast the brilliance of God's nature and the skies portray his amazing artistry' (Psalm 19:1 author's translation). So, it is a legitimate artistic and scientific enquiry to look for the shape of God in the shape of nature. When we undertake this exploration we may be surprised by what we find, and that is because it may challenge our unconscious mindset.

Our modernist human artefacts can very often be recognised by simplified straight lines, flat planes and competing opposites. Think of houses and office blocks, public buildings and commuter trains. Ornamentation is fussy and old-fashioned. Even curves are only acceptable if they are aerodynamic and can improve efficiency. Our world prefers straight-line thinking, logical steps, digital either/or categories, tidiness. The modernist mind is obsessed with control, the imposition of order and efficiency. Not surprisingly, in our personal lives we expect everything to work logically, a to b, straight-line growth, transport that works without a hitch, computers that don't crash. Even nature must be tamed and controlled to fit in with what we impose upon it.

Needless to say, it doesn't quite work like that. The builder's saying, 'There's no such thing as a simple job' is so true. Sod's law screws up our so-perfect plans; gremlins scurry among our computer cables; entropy rules – and we don't like it; we complain fiercely and look for the culprits, those who failed to make the plan work. This is what causes road rage, recrimination, fury at the delay, blame culture and a multitude of social ills. Seldom do we question the logic of the plan or the mindset that lay behind it.

Maybe, just maybe, we should ask whether our domination of nature was ever meant to work in this manner. For when we look at the pattern of the created order we find remarkably few straight lines. Instead, we find curves, lots of them; circles, ellipses, parabolas, hyperbolas, spirals, helices; nature is sexily serpentine and curvaceous! It is dominated by the wave form, up and down, in and out, ebb and flow, pulse and pause, climax and collapse. The rhythm of life.

Take a look at our shoreline environment. Note the rolling waves, the rippled sand, the sweep of the bays. This curvy, sinuous shape reveals itself just about everywhere we look from sea shells to spiral galaxies, from the way leaf nodes spiral round the stalk and flowers unfold, and the waves rise and fall on the seashore, and water ripples, and day follows night, and summer and winter, springtime and harvest; a never-ending throbbing, vibrating harmony of symbiosis. Note, too, the migratory patterns of birds, animals and fish, even the rhythmic way they move. Who is not enchanted by the swooping murmuration of starlings at sunset? It's all so much more vibrant and textured than the monolithic office block.

Even the fact that we can see this harmony and hear it is likewise dependent on the wave forms of light and of sound and the ability of our own brain waves to interpret these and make sense of our world. In fact, the electrical patterns remind us that our hearts beat to a sine curve rhythm, too. Having had problems with this because of over-fitness in younger years, I am very aware of how important this particular wave form is to my ongoing life!

Speaking of which, the very structure of life, our DNA, is a double helix, a twisted ladder. Even at this microscopic level we find the same pattern, and smaller still we see it in radioactive decay and in the shape of molecules and atoms. Go to the farthest galaxies from which some surmise that life might have originated and you will find the same pattern written throughout the universe. Even the theory of black holes indicates a constant dying and rebirth.

Understanding this has helped us to generate alternating current electricity, and the rifling of a gun barrel to spin a bullet in a helix so that it flies true, or to spin nylon thread, or make ropes and hawsers, and ten thousand other manufacturing processes, not forgetting radio waves and the entire electromagnetic spectrum that we make use of daily. In fact, as far as I can see, this coiled spring, the helical form of a three dimensional wave moving through the fourth dimension of time, is probably the one shape from which all other geometric shapes can be fashioned.

It appears then that the most natural selection is by default the helical wave form. If this is so then our straight-line approach to life is often going to be in conflict with nature. Maybe that's why the environmentally aware Christian author J.R.R. Tolkien had his hobbits living in round houses rather than rectangular ones!

Being increasingly alienated from nature our techno-modernist society does not make easy provision for its rhythms. We portray the successful life as birth, acquisition (family, fame, fortune) and retirement. Don't mention the D word! We do not take kindly to any interruption to this straight-line progression and when it is broken by accident, setback, or suffering, we seldom find healthy resources for coping. Maybe we should change our model, our paradigm of life, to understand better what is going on, especially when the rhythm is on a downturn. Maybe our governments would handle the economy better if they recognised the same rhythmical pattern.

Perhaps, too, we can spot the first glimmerings of a likely shape to God. Maybe he is the Rhythm from whom all rhythm is derived, the Beat and Heartbeat of the universe. Rock 'n' roll, God! And given the rhythms involved in love-making, he certainly would not be opposed to sex and its pleasures.

7. Two More Books

At the conclusion of my fourth children's fantasy, *Tergan's Lair*, King Oswain and his friends discover the defeated dragon's treasure in the form of a golden casket. Upon opening it, instead of the anticipated gold and jewels, they find an ancient book entitled *The Tale of the Seven Rainbows*. Oswain is delighted. This is the long lost Book of Truth, he declares. Treasure indeed!

The children are less convinced, but Joshua wants to read it. Oswain obliges reluctantly. Although a faint rainbow haze might be sensed over the pages, all Joshua can see is a boring story about people with strange names. He hands the book back with a shrug of disappointment.

Many of us are like Joshua when we encounter the second book on our quest: the Bible.

The Book Of Books

Still the world's bestselling book, translated into every major language, countless millions read it daily. As I write, the Bible app YouVersion alone has just passed 275 million installs and the world's largest hard-copy Bible publisher based in China produces some 12 million copies each year. Most readers consider it the means whereby God speaks to them – the Word of God, no less. Even some atheists consider that you are an intellectual barbarian if you fail to read this book. Together with the Greek myths, the Bible stories inform not only our language but our literature, our stories, our theatre, our art and our films. It is essential reading for anyone who wishes to understand the human condition and to reflect upon the meaning of their own life.

Your knowledge of the Bible may be limited to the selective content and the state-approved interpretation of that content that you were taught at school. We should not necessarily accept that version. Like all scientific endeavours, making new discoveries requires us to go beyond our existing knowledge and presuppositions; it is only then that the object of our investigation reveals its secrets. It takes a certain humility to do this – and a degree of risk (perhaps another word for faith). Yet what matters is not what we already see, but what we haven't yet seen. That's the point of the quest.

I did not have a religious background, so when I first opened a Bible I began to read it for what it is: a story, a narrative, a grand saga. I did not come to it with an agenda, or to prove or disprove anything. I let it say what it had to say, because this seemed to me to be intellectually honest. I recommend that you do the same.

Many people do not read the Bible honestly. They do not enquire deeply enough. They do not allow it to do what it claims to do, so they speak nonsense when it comes to discussing it, resorting to cant dismissals with words like boring, or incomprehensible, or out of date, or irrelevant. It is decidedly none of those things to anyone who will read and inquire as to its real meaning.

What I discovered was a very truthful book. It doesn't shrink from the realities of human frailty and perversity; its heroes are flawed characters; its villains sometimes do good; ordinary people sometimes do amazing things. It is a survivalist's tale of sacrifice, selfishness and greed, of sex, war and violence, some of it done in the name of God with justifiable reasons – and some of it done in the name of God with apparently unjustifiable reasons. There is love and death, adultery, murder, child abuse, rape, fraud, rebellion and falsehood, justice and injustice, all mixed in with amazing heroism, faith, beauty, courage, joy and hope and perseverance in the belief that somehow love triumphs over all the evil.

What starts out with the origin of intelligent *homo sapiens* in an idyllic garden, ends with a renewal of the entire cosmos in which we become more than we ever expected to be. For this is ultimately an optimistic book, a divine comedy that ends not with evil but with absolute goodness – the redemption of all that can be redeemed, the mending of all that can be mended, the healing of all that can be healed. In the vastness of astronomical time the short story of this little blip on a small planet comes to a happy ending with a bright new future.

So, obtain a modern English version and follow the traditional advice if you are a good reader, and start at the beginning with the book of Genesis. Or begin with part two, known as the New Testament. If you struggle with reading it then listen to an audio version. You will encounter easy bits and difficult bits, some of it boring and incomprehensible, other parts incredibly moving and inspiring. I encourage you to stick with it.

Sometimes you will find yourself agreeing, and at others disagreeing, with the comments and judgements made upon the events and personalities. They are there so that you will reflect on them and then ask yourself why you came to these opinions. For this Bible is essentially a mirror that enables us to see ourselves in the light of the possibility of God. In this sense it tests us as well as informs and educates us. It examines our emotional responses and our motives. You are meant to argue with it, to disagree, but to reflect on why you argue with it and why you disagree. If you persevere you may well find yourself revising your opinions, for it is a book that raises questions and invites us not to blind faith, but to intelligent faith.

Now, once again we are looking for a pattern as we read. You will find as with the natural world a great and a repeated waveform, or to put it three dimensionally, a spiralling or helical form, like a coiled spring. Rising, falling, rising again; or if you will, life, death, resurrection. The upturned smile of a comedy mask rather than the downturned mouth of a tragedy mask. Both are there in the

Bible but the overall pattern is clearly the comedic and optimistic.

The pattern is revealed in many of the narrative tales of individuals: Noah, who built an ark and 'died' to the old world that perished through wickedness, to start again in a washed-clean world. Abraham who waited a lifetime for an heir but offered the child to God as a sacrifice in accordance with local custom, only to have his son spared and restored to him alive. Joseph the favoured younger son with his Technicolor dream coat finding himself in an Egyptian jail on a false charge of rape but then being raised to become Minister of Agriculture; Moses adopted by Pharaoh's daughter and educated in the Egyptian royal court, fleeing as a murderer and living as a fugitive in the wilderness, then returning to lead the Exodus and becoming one of the greatest figures in world history; David the slayer of Goliath hiding from a deranged king and living a Robin Hood existence with the distressed, the debtors, and the dispossessed, but then going on to become Israel's most eminent king; Jonah the minor prophet who landed up in the belly of a big fish, but went on to prophesy in one of the great empire cities of the ancient world.

Yet all these adventures are eclipsed by the appearance of Jesus of Nazareth. This is the tale of the Son of God who abandoned the splendour of heaven, humbled himself to live as one of us, even to the point of becoming the blame-taker for all our misdeeds. Dying a cruel sacrificial death, God then raised him from the dead and promoted him to be the ruler of the universe. Life, death, resurrection; this is the pattern of redemption and, as we shall later see, is the key to understanding the nature of God and its bearing on our own afflictions.

If you get nothing more from reading the Bible than the ability to identify this pattern then you will be more than justified in making the effort and you will have taken a great step forward in understanding the meaning of life. In the words of the apostle Paul, you will have begun to be 'transformed by the renewing of your mind' (Romans 12:2) – not so much what you think but how you think.

The Book Within

The third book I have in mind is ourselves.

Ever since Arthur Hayley's 1976 novel *Roots* and the ensuing TV series, people have wanted to understand their origins and the effect that has on their own current identity. Who am I?

We are all a story in the telling; we each produce a unique tale of our time and place in history. We weave on time's canvas the things we did, what we felt, what happened to us, our joys and our sorrows, the people we loved and hated, our achievements and our losses, our hopes and dreams, our pride and our shame, our lusts and our longings.

In the West we pride ourselves on being our own persons. Individual worth, our own egos, matter more than the group, the tribe or the nation. Common cause may unite us but for the most part we and our close circle of family and friends are what counts. The fact that many of our circles are remarkably conformist to outsiders probably escapes us, especially when we are young, but that's to be expected. Few people are that unique!

What also escapes us is the fact that however individual we like to think we are, we are all subject to the same patterns, the most basic of which is that we are born, we live, and we die. Looked at negatively, we are all tragedies; from dust we were made and to dust we return. The fleeting flowering of our lives soon fades and we are gone. Depressing, isn't it?

Yet life is seldom that simple, or that bad. Within the overall rise and fall are many other rhythms, and unless we are excessively morbid in outlook, these are the ones that affect us the most on a day-to-day basis. There are the obvious ones like a woman's monthly cycle of fertility and menstruation and renewal. Or male potency leading to the fertilisation of an egg but involving the absorption (death) of the sperm to bring about new life.

Then there are the rhythms of the day: waking, working, weariness, sleep and reawakening. Or hunger, replenishment, fullness, hunger again. Desire, gratification, satisfaction, desire again. Much as we might wish it we humans cannot take unlimited, unbroken gratification, which is why pure pleasure-seeking fails and why recreational drugs like Ecstasy and cocaine cannot deliver the promise of everlasting bliss without destroying us in the process. You may get high with a little help from your friends but it will always be the law of diminishing returns because we are all constrained by the pattern of creation.

These rhythms of life follow the same pattern that we observe in nature and in the Bible: rise, fall, rise again, or life, death, resurrection, if you will. The wise person recognises this and accepts the ups and downs as part of life. Those who burn the candle at both ends burn out quickest for want of this elementary self-knowledge.

What lay behind the ancient Sabbath concept of a day off, what inspired the holy seasonal feasts that today we call holidays, was not so much religion but a recognition of entropy. We need rest and renewal to sustain life and activity. The stupidity of modern government is to imagine that we will be more productive if we never rest, that we will buy more if the shops never close, that we will be happier if the football season never ends and we can eat sour, bullet-hard strawberries in January! Little wonder we are a glutted, bored, weary society enslaved to sameness.

Events, circumstances, the unexpected, will conspire to mess all this up – and that's when we are thrown. Sudden illness, the loss of a loved one, redundancy, an accident; these things wreck the normal patterns of life and break into our expectation of stability. In the process they superimpose their own rhythms which can make our natural downers far worse and our uppers impossible to attain. It's what we call depression, or grief, and most of us are ill-prepared for it and want out of it as soon as possible. This is why we turn to antidepressants long term rather than making the journey of life, death and resurrection. I am not opposed to antidepressant medication, but taking the edge off a crisis is one thing; making that a way of life is quite another.

My point is this: our inner moods also undulate in a wave form and this may not be as bad as we think. Maybe we need the undulation to fit in with creation. Perhaps these cycles are normal and even necessary for our long-term growth and well-being. Just possibly this helical pattern, including the painful bits, is healthy after all. Could it be that even the pains are less a setback and more a process of transformation so that we might become what we were best meant to be? Well, we shall see. For the moment let's simply recognise that our lives are made up of the same rhythms, the same helical patterns that we observe in other lives, in the movements of history and in the physical universe as a whole. Even when we encounter adversity, that same pattern holds true.

Now, although the helical wave form is not the only one in the universe, it is by far the most dominant. So, what might this tell us about God? If he exists, then what shape might he be?

8. The Shape of God

I paint and draw. The biggest problem with drawing is not what we do with our hands, but how we see. Most of us see what we expect to see; we have preconceived models of what a face looks like, for example. When we attempt to draw that face our preconception dictates what we actually draw. The results are disappointing; in thinking we are copying a likeness we produce an unlikeness. We have to learn an artist's way of seeing, which at first seems that we are drawing an unlikeness but which turns out to be a likeness!

My point is: we have a default way of looking at God that produces a distortion of God, because we don't see properly and don't even know that we don't see properly. My hope is that by learning to see the true 'shape of God' we shall be able to draw a better likeness in our own lives. The apostle Paul encouraged his readers not to conform to the existing thought patterns of their culture but to be transformed by a new way of thinking. Then they would be able to grasp and experience just how good, pleasing and perfect God's purposes are (Romans 12:2). Let's remind ourselves that this is not simply a matter of what we think (education, subject matter) but how we think.

What comes to mind when we mention the shape of God? Most probably images and icons, statues of wood, metal or stone, idols that are either the objects of worship or the gateway to the worshipful Presence. Officially at least, Judaism, Christianity and Islam have no religious objects as gods or the representation of gods. Their God is invisible, and anything shaped to look like

God, let alone to be worshipped as God, is blasphemous. God is the Creator, not the created. The crucifixes and images of the saints much-loved by the Roman Catholic Church are not to be understood as objects of worship, though many Protestants and others would say that this is what they become in practice. Even so, this is a misuse of the artefacts, and religion divides quite neatly between these three 'one God' faiths, and all the rest.

The others are the polytheists like the ancient Greeks and Romans, or many modern-day Hindus who shape their gods from a variety of animal, vegetable and mineral origins. For the most part, the gods of polytheists turn out to be merely variants of ourselves. We make gods in our own image. Indeed, it is likely that over the course of history the majority of such deities were no more than the projections of strong men or sexy women, made variously beautiful or grotesque depending on whether we want to be attracted to them or wished them to repel our spiritual or earthly enemies.

What fascinates me about the Judaeo-Christian God, Yahweh, is that he is not a projection of our human aspirations, lusts or militarism. He is so totally Other, so different from us. This is why Sigmund Freud's God as an 'old man in the sky', idealised father projection, breaks down as an argument. God is so different from us or our fathers. If fatherhood it is, then it is most unlike any earthly fatherhood. If he is just an idealised man then he is not what we would look for or invent.

For human-like gods we would turn to the Greeks and to Mount Olympus. Those gods most manifestly are a projection of our human desires and passions. In many ways they serve the purpose of a modern soap opera, allowing us to reflect on human morals and conduct. For example, the goddess Nemesis exacts retribution on those who show arrogance, hubris, before the gods. This thought is found in the Bible, also. 'Pride goes before destruction, a haughty spirit before a fall' (Proverbs 16:18). This observation remains remarkably true of human nature to this day and cautions us to remember that our actions have consequences.

Turning to the Bible perspective on God, we find he has no physical shape; he is enshrined in no idol. So, when I speak about the shape of God, I am not talking in physical terms. I am not even referring primarily to his moral shape – which is love – but to his essential nature. My proposition is that there is a vital core shape to God. It is one that at the street level we have forgotten or ignored, but one that goes a long way towards answering some of our biggest questions about God and the cosmos. For the shape of God must fundamentally determine the kind of universe we inhabit, physically, morally and spiritually. It must define beyond local custom and culture that which is universal to all existence. It should bring together science, art, spirituality, philosophy and ethics in a kind of Grand Unified Theory that helps us make sense of our lives and society.

Most people who know me have never actually met me. They have discovered me through my writings, paintings and recordings. They don't know me intimately as my family and close friends do, but from my works they can deduce a reasonable idea of what I am and am not like. Our observation of the three 'books' can achieve the same end when it comes to God. In particular, we must look at the pattern. Concentrating on the details will leave us confused.

When we look at this big life, death, resurrection pattern, the pattern of nature, of the Bible narrative and of our own selves, we begin to realise a fundamental rhythm to how the universe operates. It follows that God must in some sense be characterised by the same rhythm as the universe he created.

Paddling in the shallows of ever-moving water and sand helps us loosen free from the too easy rigid dualisms and contradictions, the either/ors, of our culture. At the shoreline we are on land and also in the sea. It's a both/and environment, and it is flexible. But there's no mistaking its helical or spiral nature. It immediately challenges us to think three dimensionally with no sharp corners or fixity. The universe is on a roll and God must be in some sense helical. Only a God like this would have made a world like this.

Mention life, death and resurrection and Christians will immediately think they are on safe ground. After all, isn't this the story of Christ? Granted, but surely the nature of God has to be viewed as more than a brief blip in time. It must be eternal and be intrinsic to what God is always like. Once we really grasp this we will understand far better what God can and what God can't do, as well as what he will or won't do.

The Pattern of Three

A helix is a three-dimensional shape, like a coiled spring, or a screw thread. As a painter I have to convert three-dimensional images into the two-dimensions of a canvas, using all sorts of visual tricks to give the illusion of depth and perspective. How much simpler for the potter or sculptor who works with the given three dimensions! In art and photography the most satisfying composition usually involves three objects. Somehow threes produce a sense of harmony, completeness, enough but not too much. Two form a pair but it takes three to form a family or community. Even at the level of the atom our primary particles that constitute matter are three bound together as an oscillating force field: proton, electron and neutron. An artist's palette needs just three primary colours to make all others: magenta, cyan and yellow. Even we ourselves may be described as body, soul and spirit. Three turns up wherever we look, it seems, right down to the internal combustion engine, and right up to the nuclear power of the stars.

Of particular interest to us is the fact that binary or dualistic thinking can only produce a straight line of opposing poles. Dualism of that kind has characterised the West for centuries. It explains our polarised society, our extremists and fundamentalists, our disagreements and dogmatisms. And that makes it all the harder for us to understand what God is like.

Three poles turn a straight line into a triangle. In doing so they create a single area or a zone, a realm of activity. We can see, too, that this pattern of three fits our dynamic helical life, death, resurrection pattern.

I have never been too happy with the idea that God is unchanging, if by that we imagine a frozen fresco in the sky, an impassive stern-faced monarchical presence, a greater power that is just sort of there like digestive biscuits or porridge oats, or Mount Everest, or granny in the corner. Certainly this should not be a Christian concept of God. The God presented in the Bible and reflected in nature is energetic, interactive, and pulsating with life and power.

The Bible consistently draws a distinction between man-made idols and the living God. The prophet Isaiah, for example, mocks the stupidity of the man who takes a piece of tree trunk, laboriously carves it into the shape of a god, then uses the shavings to cook his lunch before bowing down to a useless block of wood in worship! It's hard to say who is the biggest blockhead, the hunk of wood or the idiot worshipping it! (Isaiah 44:9–20).

That is not to say there aren't hints in ancient paganism. The Celts celebrated the Winter solstice as a dying and rebirth of the sun. Their observation of the seasons and their relationship to the position of the sun and the length of the days was valid science. Their deification of the sun was a mistake but their recognition of the cycle of life, death and rebirth was not. This is perhaps why the Celtic Christians sculpted their stone crosses with the circle of the seasons haloed around the crux. For them there was no discontinuity between the natural world and the world of redemption; the death of Christ contains within it also the resurrection, as sure as the turning of the seasons.

Likewise, the Eastern religious concept of reincarnation, even though it is not the same as resurrection, does at least hint at the possibility of dying and rebirth.

There is a toy that I sometimes use as a visual aid. It is called a Slinky and it is best known as a long coiled spring made of flattened metal strip whose main play function is to be placed at the top of the stairs and allowed to 'walk' to the bottom. Not exactly PlayStation, but still fun for kids. For me this helical shape allows me to illustrate the life, death, resurrection cycle. Joined end to end the Slinky creates a torus shape, like the circular windings on a ring magnet or a doughnut. It provides a simple but powerful illustration of life energy continually rising and falling.

Now we have to be careful when describing God as a geometric shape. The best this can be is a 'personality pattern' based upon our observations from those three 'books'. Like art, it is a metaphor; it does not exactly describe the reality. Instead it is a guidepost.

God is not made of metal. Nor is he held in our hands. I would need to expand my Slinky to infinity and I would have to set everything that was, is and is to come within its compass – and I would need to energise the entire construct with life and personality. So much for the limits of visual aids. God is God and we see only what we may. The Slinky is not to be worshipped. At best it is an aid to visualising the metaphor that reveals the personality of God.

This should not throw us. Colour itself, even the names of colours, are metaphors to describe our optical ability to see a small part of the electromagnetic spectrum. But objects do not have colour. A red balloon absorbs all other parts of the visible spectrum except red. That's what we detect and then give it a name that is used for all sorts of other metaphors. A 'blood' orange, passion red, seeing red, red rag to a bull, Red Nose Day, and so on. An artist's palette consisting of just the three primary colours allows us to paint the Sistine Chapel or *The Scream*, both of which point to greater though very different aspects of reality, but both works of art are metaphors.

We use metaphors all the time as humans. As we have seen, the big bang is just one way of expressing a start to the universe. A black hole is another metaphor, as is dark matter. Even the term 'planet' means wanderer because the Greek astronomers thought that's what the heavenly bodies did.

Whatever the ultimate reality of God is like, he remains a mystery, indeed *the* Mystery that we can only really describe in word pictures. That doesn't mean he is not real; it's just that our finite minds are struggling to describe the infinite.

Just to remind us, shortly before his death, Isaac Newton said, 'I do not know what I may appear to the world; but to myself I seem to have been only like a boy, playing on the seashore, and diverting myself in now and then finding a smoother pebble or a prettier shell than ordinary, while the great ocean of truth lay all undiscovered before me.'[6] Humility is a prerequisite to true learning.

The Trinity

This pattern of three in unity and motion was not lost on the early Christians as they came to terms with a unique experience so profound that it would change their entire world view and produce a faith like no other. It would come to be known as Trinitarian.

The first followers of Jesus Christ faced a dilemma. All their evidence and experience indicated that God possessed personality, that he was truly alive, and had revealed himself as Father, as Son, as Holy Spirit. Until then you either believed in one God, as did the Jews, or you believed in many gods, as did everyone else. This raised immediate questions. Was God three Gods? Evidently not. The Christians believed in one Creator and Sustainer of all things. But if he is not plural, how can Jesus be God, and how can the Holy Spirit be God? And which one do you pray to? Father, Son or Holy Spirit?

Central to the Christian story is the reality of God the Father revealing himself among us as Jesus, the Son of God, i.e. God's revealed form. Further, that when Jesus returned to heaven, God's way of remaining in the world would be by his Holy Spirit present in human lives. This was by no means an abstract concept, nor simply the historic experience of the first followers; it was normal Christian experience from the very beginning. It became a problem only when they tried to explain it in logical terms!

The issue resolved itself by around AD 350 with the use of two words. The first, and best known, is the word Trinity. This unique usage explained that God is one essential Being who consists of three Persons, or realities, described as Father, Son and Holy Spirit. Crudely we parallel this use of language when we describe a human being as consisting of a distinguishable body, soul and spirit, yet still being one individual.

Christianity is not monotheistic in the way Islam or Judaism are. It was monotheism that killed Christ! Nor is it polytheistic as Hinduism is. Nor is God the impersonal Absolute as with Buddhism. This is often clumsily expressed diagrammatically as the Father is not the Son or the Spirit but is God; the Son is not the Father or the Spirit but is God; the Spirit is not the Father or the Son but is God. Paintings and drawings abound. Here is one of my own based on wheels within one wheel.

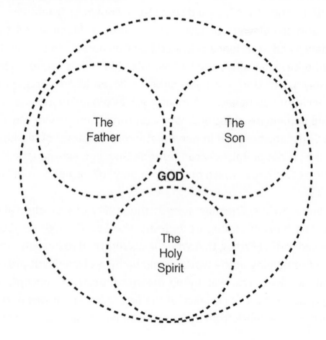

The word Trinity resolved many problems but because it was framed in the context of logical definitions it could leave us with a statement of orthodox belief but with no life to it.

The other needed but much neglected word is *perichoresis*. This Greek word means a circle dance. This is a creative way of expressing what believers knew from the Bible and in experience to be true. God is a living relationship, a loving community, within his corporate self, and he seeks to share that relationship with all creation and especially with us. The divine dance whirls and pulsates with eternal life, light and fire, a throbbing passion of love beyond anything we can imagine. For God is Love.

This all-powerful dance of eternal love and life, the sinuous interweaving of the three aspects of God in a spiritual or mystical triple helix is the root of all reality. It shifts our view of reality away from Aristotle's priority of materialism to the Bible's priority of relationship. Love becomes the heart of existence, rather than militarism, greed and oppression.

Allow ourselves to be embraced in the divine dance and our world will be transformed.

9. Justice

Have you ever watched the wild, exhilarating, swooping and whirling of a kite flying over the beach? Perhaps you can imagine one right now. This glorious freedom of the wind, its patterns sometimes predictable but most often not, tells us more about the likely nature of God than any theological textbook is ever likely to. God is wild, his love is untameable and unconstrained by our whims and fancies and neat formulae. As John's Gospel puts it, 'The wind blows wherever it pleases. You hear its sound, but you cannot tell where it comes from or where it is going' (John 3:8).

This mystical reality of the Trinity will never be boring or altogether predictable. In response to hearing that Aslan was a lion, Susan exclaims, 'I'd thought he was a man. Is he quite safe? I shall feel rather nervous about meeting a lion . . .'

'Safe?' said Mr Beaver, '. . . Who said anything about safe? 'Course he isn't safe. But he's good. He's the King, I tell you.'[7]

Trinity God isn't a man like us that we can tame and add to our apps on a smartphone. We cannot press an icon to make him do our bidding at our convenience. That's why shopping lists of prayer requests don't work, nor religious so-called cosmic commanding, or any other manipulative technique that fools us into thinking that we are in control. Try taming a spiritual supernova!

Yet passionate as God's love might be, it is not random. God is committed to restoring a relationship with us. But how can this be so if he can only frighten the living daylights out of us?

There is a large sign up ahead, like one of those that advises you of 'dangerous currents', or 'naturist beach', or 'to the Bar'. This one is a quotation from the prophet Micah. It reads, 'He has shown you, O mortal, what is good. And what does the LORD require of you? To act justly and to love mercy and to walk humbly with your God' (Micah 6:8).

Justice, mercy, humility. You will have noticed, naturally, that this is another of those patterns of three. These three fundamental virtues tell us what constitutes goodness, or love.

Now, since God declares these to represent the good life, we may assume that they are characteristics of God himself. That he desires these in us who are created in his image implies that he, too, from whom we derive that image is just, merciful, and humble.

At this point some Christians might think to equate justice, humility and mercy with the Father, Son, and Holy Spirit. That would be neat but mistaken. God manifested in three forms, as in the Trinity, is still one God and he must share all his attributes equally. That is precisely how we find it in the Bible. Father, Son and Holy Spirit are all involved in the first act of justice which is the creation of the physical laws that produced and sustain our universe.

Likewise, Father, Son and Holy Spirit reveal grace and mercy where we might merit none but dare to ask, anyway. And the same goes for humility. That God communicates with us, hears our prayers and desires a relationship with us reveals a divine humility. Otherwise he, having no needs, would have nothing to do with us.

All this was made explicit in Jesus' life. He exercises his rule over the elements; he shows mercy to the sick, the outcast and the penitent, and he humbles himself in death for the sake of others. Justice, mercy, humility – the three virtues of a God of love.

Now imagine these three virtues forming an inverted triangle. A simple diagram will make it clear.

Now we can label the points of the triangle as I have done: justice, mercy and, at the bottom, humility. Compare this with life, death, resurrection and you will have an approximation of what I mean by up, down and up again. The eternal essence of God, his shape, is justice, humility, and mercy – the same pattern that we find throughout the created order, in the Christian gospel, and even in ourselves, if we will.

That area, zone, realm, is the world of love and grace. It is as vast as the universe and as personal as our individual lives.

However, geometric symbols are of limited value. Justice, mercy and humility only take on meaning when we apply them to personalities and relationships. In this case we are considering our possible relationship with Trinity God.

So, let's start with the justice of God.

Justice and Law

What images do our minds conjure up when we hear the word justice? First and foremost, we probably think of the law and courtrooms – a world that is alien to most of us law-abiding citizens. Listen to our news media and you will soon learn that justice can be hard to come by – unless you have shed loads of money, and then it seems you can get away with almost anything!

Wronged people often cry out for justice, as famously in the Hillsborough disaster, noted for charges of police cover-ups and media distortions. On a much wider canvas, millions of people are denied justice across the globe. People are unjustly persecuted, denied human rights, deprived of their land, livelihoods and personal freedom. In the West we have made great progress in linking justice with human rights and equality yet, in spite of centuries of progress, the world is still appallingly unequal.

Human justice is usually enshrined in fair laws applicable to all. Without the rule of law society collapses into anarchy. Imagine trying to drive on a crowded island like Great Britain if there were no traffic laws. It can be bad enough with laws! Or what if anyone could mint their own currency and print their own credit cards. At these levels most of us believe that justice is a good and necessary thing.

Likewise, at the level of science we recognise the importance of the laws of nature, in particular, the fundamental constants upon which the universe as we know it appears to depend. For example, without the gravitational constant we would not be able to put up satellites for our communication systems, or fly aeroplanes, or even get out of bed safely.

These laws of contingency, however, may also allow the existence of evils such as cancer; yet they also permit the development of effective treatments. Nuclear weapons are morally abhorrent yet nuclear medicine can save lives; the same laws make both options possible. The Internet has created the greatest reservoir of knowledge and communication we have ever known, yet it also can be the vehicle for dehumanising pornography, hate mail, gratuitous violence, spam, viruses, fraud and deception. That's contingency for you!

Now if God is the Creator he is also the source of these remarkable laws. 'The works of his hands are faithful and just; all his precepts are trustworthy. They are established for ever and ever, enacted in faithfulness and uprightness' (Psalm 111:7–8).

So far, so good.

Our problems with God's justice arise when we are told that he will judge our personal morality. Immediately we feel alienated because we know we have failed any standard of perfection that might be applied to us. Despair lies at the heart of our God-avoidance. Imagine on our journey you were to come across two slabs of engraved stone half submerged on the shore. You pull them out, clean them up and read the following:

1. The Big Guy rules. OK.
2. Stick with the Big Guy alone and your team wins.
3. Respect. Don't mouth off about the Big Guy.
4. Everyone take Saturday off to relax.
5. Look after the old folks or you won't get to be one.
6. Don't go round killing people, accidentally or on purpose.
7. Don't mess about with someone else's spouse.
8. If you ain't paid for it, put it back.
9. Don't drop other people in the poo by telling lies.
10. Play with your own toys and leave other people's alone.

You realise, of course, that you have come across a version (mine) of Moses' Ten Commandments. You'll find the 'formal' version recorded in Exodus 20:3–17. Have you kept them all perfectly? I certainly haven't and I have no way of atoning for my past misdemeanours. The law by itself can only condemn me to failure and presumably judgement. So why even try?

These laws formed the basis for the national identity of the emergent nation of Israel. They were a legal contract that governed people's relationship with God and their relationship with one another. As such they described the basis on which God would relate to them. This was not as cold-blooded as it sounds. The love of God lay at its heart and the agreement was commonly pictured as both the relationship between child and parent, and also as a marriage between husband and wife. A society that kept these laws would be characterised by trust, an absence of religious conflict, honour for God that affected our relationship with each other, and no aggressive bad language. It would enjoy a national holiday every week, old people would be cared for without resentment. Murder and adultery would cease and families would stay together. There would be no shoplifting, nor Internet fraud, no burglars. Everyone would tell the honest truth and we would meet our needs without greed. Not bad!

The subsequent history of Israel as recorded in the Bible demonstrated eloquently that this covenant didn't work. God might be faithful and true, but human beings are incapable of living rightly. Israel proved repeatedly guilty of rebellion and spiritual adultery that led in its turn to political and religious corruption. As a result, the nation endured exile and forfeited its political autonomy. By the time Jesus came on the scene the living relationship with God had been replaced by a multitude of petty laws and regulations. Spiritual health and safety gone mad! Vital faith had degenerated into mere religion with its endless cycle of guilt, atonement and more guilt. Even that ceased when in AD 70 the Temple was destroyed by the Romans once and for all.

That strand of the justice of God has much to teach us by way of example and analogy, but we should not subject ourselves to its strictures. Non-Jewish people are not bound by that old covenant. If we tried it we would fail, so there is no point in doing so.

Here's the good news. We were never expected to live that kind of perfect life. Applying a national legal code of conduct to our personal behaviour would always lead us astray. It would either condemn us every day or, wherever we did succeed, make us inordinately proud, or, of course, terribly deceitful!

One of the greatest experts at keeping the law was Saul of Tarsus. Later in his life he recalled his experience:

Circumcised on the eighth day, of the people of Israel, of the tribe of Benjamin, a Hebrew of Hebrews; in regard to the law, a Pharisee; as for zeal, persecuting the church; as for righteousness based on the law, faultless. But whatever were gains to me I now consider loss for the sake of Christ. What is more, I consider everything a loss because of the surpassing worth of knowing Christ Jesus my Lord, for whose sake I have lost all things. I consider them garbage, that I may gain Christ. (Philippians 3:5–8)

Paul, as he became known, had discovered the futility of religion, of believing in a God who set an impossibly high standard, knowing we couldn't achieve it and then sending us all to hell for failing the exam. That is not a God of love who wants a relationship with us! If God is love then the justice of God must mean that he is on our side. So his law is good and designed for our well-being and protection, not for our destruction. The Ten Commandments are not arbitrary rules governed by God's whims and fancies but laws that turn out to be for our benefit. Jesus summed up the Ten Commandments in just two: 'You shall love the Lord your God with all your heart, soul and mind, and you shall love your neighbour as yourself' (see Matthew 22:37–40). The apostle Paul simply stated that 'love is the fulfilment of the law' (Romans 13:10).

Most of the Bible references to the theme of justice are not about God threatening to beat us up if we don't behave better; they are instead about celebrating his justice. The words come from the lips of the oppressed and persecuted, the poor and down-trodden. God reveals that he has a special place in his heart for such people. No surprise then that judgement, even hell, if you will, is reserved for those who create hell for others. The rulers of this world, the power brokers, the evil-minded in high places are first in line to reap what they have sown. The message is clear, if you relieve the plight of the needy, make peace, ensure fairness, treat others as you would wish to be treated yourself, then you too will reap what you have sown. Generally we call this heaven.

We should question why we mock the notion of a day of judgement. Are we deep down so scared that we must pretend it doesn't exist? Or have we totally misunderstood the Bible? Does our dud street paradigm of a distant God really mean that what we fear is relentless law being applied to our fallible lives when he catches up with us? So we deny that possibility, lodge our self-righteous defences in advance; driven by despair we hope that we simply snuff it at the end and that's all there is to it.

Love lies at the heart of justice. God rules the nations with this kind of justice, a justice that springs from love – because God is love. He expects us to do the same and if we don't, then watch out! This is what the Bible is getting at when it says that Jesus will rule the nations with a rod of iron. This does not mean he is a cruel tyrant but that he holds to an unbending standard by which nations and individuals are judged. Do you rule your sphere of influence with a heart of love for others? If you do then your actions and decisions will be just. If you don't then you are abusing the position God has allowed you to hold.

So, justice is about social ethics. The person, government or institution that behaves unjustly is also unrighteous, that is, morally corrupt and guilty of failing to love their neighbour as themselves. This has profound implications for how we do business, especially at a multinational level. It means the bottom line of profit cannot be treated as an unqualified absolute, whatever it costs others. Good business and government acts for the common good of the people, staff, resource suppliers, the environment, customers and shareholders alike. It is relational and seeks to nurture an environment of health and wealth for all. That is only fair.

It's time to look at the next aspect of God's nature.

10. Mercy

The seashore is not always a kind place of beauty and refreshment. Hurricanes, tsunamis, and the like, can wreak devastation and leave many destitute and homeless. Victims of these disasters need mercy in the most practical of ways: food, shelter, medical care, protection.

I equate mercy with resurrection because to receive mercy is to receive a new and better life. If, for example, I am a starving refugee and somebody shows mercy to me by providing me with shelter, food and health care, then I have a fresh start in life. If I am a thief because I am driven by drug addiction, and the court instead of simply punishing me by sending me to prison, provides me with a way of curing my addiction, then that mercy has resurrected my life. If one has fallen into adultery through an act of weakness or folly and is truly repentant, their life partner has every right to dump them, but if that wronged spouse receives them back (and there is no obligation that they should) then the marriage might experience a resurrection into something new and better as a result of that mercy.

Mercy is not a weak virtue. It is an act of power on behalf of the vulnerable. The merciful one uses their position of strength or superiority to bring kindness to those who need it, whether they deserve it or not. Don't you just hate those patronising terms, 'the deserving poor' or 'those less fortunate than ourselves'? Mercy is not dispassionate charity and it does not demean the recipient. There is no sense of 'you should think yourself lucky' and nor should it depend on the depth of grovelling and begging on the part of the supplicant.

True mercy is a disposition of the heart that seeks to empower and enrich, to restore and advance those who are in need. It is for their benefit, not for that of the one showing mercy.

In general terms God reveals his mercy in the cycle of the seasons. The story of Noah and his ark marks a death of the old world as a judgement on its extraordinary corruption. Noah, his family, and the animals are 'buried' in a huge floating coffin until the rain ceases and the volcanic activity dies down. As the flood waters recede and the sun reappears Noah's family and all biological life forms are promised providential mercy:

> Never again will I curse the ground because of humans, even though every inclination of the human heart is evil from childhood. And never again will I destroy all living creatures, as I have done. As long as the earth endures, seedtime and harvest, cold and heat, summer and winter, day and night will never cease. (Genesis 8:21–22)

Whenever we see a rainbow it reminds us of God's mercy towards this planet. In spite of occasional localised upsets and modest cycles of warming and cooling, the biosphere is remarkably stable, the seasons are reliable (in the UK, cool and damp!), there are no wild polar swings or orbital wobbles, and the earth can produce enough food for everyone so that civilisations can develop and human activity flourish. We call this God's providence. Perhaps it's not such a bad thing to say grace before meals, instead of just taking it all for granted. Even 'Ta, Pa,' is better than nothing!

God's mercy is also revealed in his awareness of our human frailty. We are dust and to dust we shall return; we are short-lived, thin-skinned creatures, never more than a few heartbeats from death. Not only that, we are morally fallible; we do wrong, we fall short of our own standards, let alone any that God might set. Yet

God is generous with his mercy towards us. He acts like a good father, not a harsh judge. This is how one lyricist put it:

He does not treat us as our sins deserve
　or repay us according to our iniquities.
For as high as the heavens are above the earth,
　so great is his love for those who fear him;
as far as the east is from the west,
　so far has he removed our transgressions from us.
As a father has compassion on his children,
　so the LORD has compassion on those who fear him;
for he knows how we are formed,
　he remembers that we are dust. (Psalm 103:10–14)

It may be hard to understand sometimes, but God is on our side – unless we choose him not to be.

Why we should make such a ludicrous choice against his love is a matter to consider quite soon in our journey, but at the moment we are concerned with what God is like. What we learn is that creation itself was an act of joyful, exuberant love on the part of the Trinity. As we would expect, it was 'very good'. The highest expression of that creation is ourselves. We bear the 'image' of God. That makes us of infinite worth, every single one of us.

Now it is inconceivable that God would love those whom he parented any less than we love our own offspring. In fact, the psalmist indicates that God puts us together in our mother's womb. We are aware from research that our DNA does not follow a rigid programme but adapts and shapes according to factors that we cannot predict. Humans are not clones. This ancient understanding anticipates modern genetics by some 3000 years! Here's the quote:

For you formed my inward parts;
you knitted me together in my mother's womb.

I praise you, for I am awesomely and wonderfully made.
Wonderful are your works;
my soul knows it very well.
My structure was not hidden from you,
when I was being made in secret,
intricately woven in the depths of the womb.
Your eyes oversaw my developing embryo.
(Psalm 139:13–16 author's translation)

Why things sometimes go wrong is a matter we will address later as part of a wider issue. For the moment let's recognise that all children are loved and accepted by God from the beginning of their existence. And they are all born innocent of intent or action. There are no demon babies!

Any child that dies in this pre-ego state goes straight to heaven. Of that I am certain.

As we all know, that innocence does not last. The fall of humanity, expressed so well in the story of Adam and Eve, whether we believe it was literal or otherwise, tells the truth about human nature. But there is another version, too, and it goes by the name of the Parable of the Prodigal Son. Jesus told it like this:

A father had two much-loved sons, both of whom rebelled against his love as their egos developed, but in very different ways. The first, now of age, demanded his share of the bountiful estate. The father let him have his inheritance, whereupon the boy left home and squandered it all on wild living until he had bankrupted his soul as well as his assets. He was reduced to slave labour. At this point he came to his senses and in an act of humility decided he might as well slave for his father as for anyone else. He might even be lucky to get that. After all, he had humiliated his family, wasted hard-earned resources, become a moral reprobate. However, it turned out that the father had been waiting for his son's return and instead of disowning him, which was what the son deserved, he threw the boy a welcome home party. The father showed mercy and the son received a resurrection.

The other son despised his father in a more subtle way. All the time fearing that he might be rejected for not meeting the performance targets, he spent his life in hard duty, rule-keeping and self-denial. Never once did his stoicism allow him to enjoy the blessings of the estate. Not surprisingly, he was outraged when his father welcomed back his reprobate brother.

The story is universal in its application, as witness a multitude of books and films that carry the theme. *Les Miserables* being just one. We human beings, so blessed by God's gifts, decide it's all ours by right and we squander it. In the process we distance ourselves from God until maybe we come to our senses. Fearing only judgement, we have low expectations of any resurrection after our fall.

Meanwhile the religious rule-keepers live in constant doubt about God's love and believe only stern duty can keep us on the straight and narrow. They never party with God. The Trinitarian dance is alien to their killjoy religion.

Lurching between the poles of legalism and license we fail to understand God's love and his freely given mercy. He is longing to forgive us of both kinds of folly, if only we will let him. Our problem is that we see self-indulgence or self-denial as the only two options. Typical dualistic thinking! God's third option is relationship with him and that opens up a whole new vista of experience, an arena of grace and love that is communal, creative, delightful, joyful and pure without regrets or repression.

Grace is the mercy of God towards people who have failed to love God and one another. Those who have fallen short of the standard may deserve judgement but instead can receive a forgiveness that is freely offered to all who want it. That not everyone wants it is another story which we will touch on later, but God's mercy is unconditionally offered and no one is disqualified from applying, including you and me.

Let's be clear on this, Jesus as the revelation of God in human form, whom Christians call the Son of God, did not come to see how many people he could condemn to hell. 'For God did not send his Son into the world to condemn the world, but to save the world through him' (John 3:17). Nor did he come to launch a religion called Christianity. That would be a very small-minded project for the eternal Logos, the creative living Word of God, the universal anointed one that we call Christ, through whom everything originated. Jesus wants the entire prodigal human race back in relationship with God. To achieve that, he came to abolish religion as a form of rules and regulations, rituals and sacrifices, and to replace it with grace.

It goes even further than that. As the Christ he intends to reconcile the entire damaged cosmos, to complete the life, death resurrection cycle on a cosmic scale. That is why he is described as the Alpha and the Omega, the beginning and the end. Paul expresses it like this:

> For God was pleased to have all his fullness dwell in him, and through him to reconcile to himself all things, whether things on earth or things in heaven, by making peace through his blood, shed on the cross. (Colossians 1:19–20)

The full extent of mercy will be seen in the renewal of the entire universe into something even greater.

Lest we feel a little overawed by such a purpose and wonder at our own insignificance, Jesus came to make it intimately personal. That's why he came into the world. Jesus loved to tell little stories and anecdotes that go by the name of parables. In one of them he described a religious self-righteous man who paraded his merits before God, and most impressive they were. Nearby stood another man, a bent government official who regularly ripped people off. He couldn't lift up his head for shame and could only pray, 'God, have mercy on me, a sinner.' He was the one who received mercy and forgiveness because that's what he asked for. The religious man got nothing because that's what he asked for. One experienced a spiritual resurrection and joined the cosmic dance – call it a new birth if you like – while the other dug his own grave with a shovel made of pride. The same offer is made to all of us. Which brings us neatly to our third characteristic of God.

11. Humility

As we journey along our beach we come across a number of palm trees. They are a great example of ternary or three-way thinking. Take two strong and opposed forces. One is the rigidity and fixity of a woodland tree trunk. The other is a hurricane force wind. In 1987, when I lived in South East England, overnight storm winds reached over 110 miles per hour. I ventured out in the morning to find blown apart garages and lofts and trees felled onto cars. In all, we lost some 15 million trees that did not possess sufficient flexibility to handle the storm. Palm trees are different; they regularly survive far worse storms not only because of deep tap roots but because they have the flexibility to bend fully with the wind. It's a form of humility that proves to be remarkably powerful. Yet we find it difficult to recognise this third force.

Our classical Western mindset is largely divided between Aristotle's materialism and Plato's mysticism, and that has created a culture of dualistic, binary, yes-no, true-false, for-or-against thinking. For example, in the realm of politics, parties often divide between the left and the right – in Britain, Labour and Conservative; in America, Democrats and Republicans.

Morally, most of us find ourselves sitting somewhat uneasily on a straight line between two poles when it comes to good and evil. So, if Mother Teresa is our recent icon for good and Jimmy Savile our icon for evil, then we locate ourselves and others somewhere midway on the line. From that, we determine how much justice we are entitled to, and how much mercy; and opinions will always be divided. So, the victims of crime will feel the sentence is too light, and the mother of 'he's a good boy really' will feel it is too severe.

Applied to God, this mindset has led some people to suppose that God is bipolar, that he lives with a tension between justice and mercy and sometimes flips irrationally and inconsistently from one mode to another and back again. So our prayers for justice or mercy might depend on what mood we catch him in!

The fault lies in our own two-pole thinking, our 'he loves me, he loves me not' mindset about God. The helical model of God's nature resolves this dilemma, because although God's nature is one, it is expressed in three aspects, as we have seen earlier.

Between the life and the resurrection, lies the death. Between justice and mercy is humility. Instead of a straight line we have this inverted triangle, or downward loop. We have a zone, an area or, better, a realm that takes us into a radically different way of looking at life. In this model, humility is the transition phase that takes us from religion to grace – a three-dimensional world where love is perfectly expressed and experienced in the harmony of justice, mercy and humility. This is how we are meant to live, but if we want to we must abandon our dualistic, conflicting and contradictory first life and embrace the humility that allows us into the grace of our second life.

Humility is the missing dimension in our map of reality. In fact, it's a word that we don't much like because we misunderstand what it means. Instead of seeing humility as a strength we interpret it as weakness. Typically, we balk at the notion of turning the other cheek, of letting an argument go. To us it is mealy-mouthed compliance with evil, or not standing up for our rights, not showing solidarity. Seldom do we view it as the path of wisdom and even less do we see it as the key to our personal growth, particularly through times of adversity.

So, what do we mean by humility? Furthermore, is it not blasphemous to say that God is humble as well as just and merciful? Most of our uses of the word are derogatory. Meekness equals weakness; to be humbled is to be humiliated; or the false humility expressed as 'in my humble opinion', or someone having low self-esteem. None of these may be applied to God, nor should they be applied to us. Humility is the powerful choice to disempower oneself. It is not grovelling to get your own way; nor is it surrendering to coercion or cruelty. In other words it is not compelled but selected. Humiliation is inflicted, but humility is chosen.

The meaning of the word comes from 'humus', meaning organic fertile soil. Humus is the means of producing harvests; it's what feeds us. The power of the soil lies in its ability to receive and to germinate and to nourish. This is what the apostle James had in mind when he wrote: 'receive with meekness the implanted word, which is able to save your souls' (James 1:21 NKJV). Contrast this with hard ground which the seed simply bounces off and fails to germinate. Put simply, the proud are fruitless and the humble produce harvests. That was the point of Jesus' famous parable of the sower (Matthew 13:1–23), and perhaps why the meek do 'inherit the earth'.

This 'upside-down thinking' seems strange to our ears because we are so used to the two-pole straight-line conflict mode of thought. To lose our lives that we might find them puzzles us. Yet, as artists understand, the ability to surrender our control of the subject, to go beyond what we think we should paint to painting what it is actually saying, is key to producing genuine art. In the sciences, most of the great discoveries come when we break the binary logic of current knowledge and take a 'foolish' step, one that requires humility of mind in order to do so. Mediation skills depend on the mediator not taking sides but taking the humble role that creates an environment for reconciliation. The referee is not the star, and is usually the most reviled person on the pitch, but without the ref there could be no game.

In my model, humility is represented by the lower point of the inverted triangle and is synonymous with the 'death' aspect of the helix. This being so, humility is, as with the virtues of justice and mercy, the third great characteristic of God's nature.

God is love and love is humble.

Think about this for a moment: giving and receiving love is only possible for vulnerable people because love requires not only sacrifice but also the need and the desire for completeness. This means humbly admitting that we are not complete of ourselves. The hard-hearted, the self-sufficient, can never truly love or receive love. Ultimately, they can only create their own self-isolating hell.

Trinity God exists as a perfectly integrated community of Father, Son and Holy Spirit. The divine helix consists in the synergy between justice, mercy and humility. So how does the humility of God express itself?

Most Christians will immediately think of the death of Christ and his willing choice to surrender himself to the cross. Before we come to that, let's take a step back.

If God's self-sufficiency did not include the element of humility then there could be no created world. The choice to create would not be there, and even less so to create humans in his own image. Love desires an object to love outside of oneself even if 'oneself' is a Trinity. Creation is an act of giving, of sacrifice, of paying the price for our love, despite knowing the hassle we would cause.

Then consider the matter of prayer, of communication. A proud autonomous God would not need prayer, would not agree to respond to our requests, would not discuss his plans with us, certainly would not change his mind as a result of a conversation with us. A humble God, one whose essential nature includes the 'death' aspect will do precisely that. Some go further and say that when God created time he constrained his own eternity, he emptied himself of detailed foreknowledge so that he does not know all the future. That helps us understand why our prayers matter, why our choices have such power for good or ill.

Any clear, honest reading of the Bible will reveal that there is a certain wondrous vulnerability within the nature of God. The Holy Spirit who created the world can also be grieved. Jesus wept. The

Father longs for his prodigal children to return to him. Likewise, God rejoices over us; his heart sings with delight. He takes pleasure in his works of creation like an artist or an engineer satisfied with a good job well done. God has emotions. Biochemistry may play a significant part in our emotions, but the very existence of emotions owes its origin to God himself.

In Deuteronomy 32:18 there is a Hebrew term translated as 'fathered you'. The word also carries the nuance of 'danced with you' or 'dandled you'. As we have already noted, the early church theologians used the Greek word *perichoresis* (from which we get choreography, to dance around) to describe the relationship within the Trinity. My helical dance fits this quite nicely! Creation then is a stage on which we people made in the image of God are invited to join in the sacred dance. That is the essence of celebration: worship as sheer fun, passion, joy and fulfilment. God is humble and gracious enough to let us join in with him. Celtic art with its unending knots and braids carries something of the same idea.

Like so many others in our society my concept of God was once one of awesome, irresistible power. God was a theological nuclear furnace. Approach if you dare but expect to be destroyed like the moth in the flame. My journey enabled me to realise that I had a Father in heaven who actually liked his children and the last thing he wished to do was to drive them away. It dawned on me that God has loved me for the whole of my existence, long before I realised it.

The humility of God reaches its most absolute expression in the eternal Logos (the Word) becoming human in the person we know as Jesus of Nazareth or simply Jesus Christ. The apostle Paul describes the helical wave form of life, death and resurrection perfectly with these words:

> Jesus Christ, sharing the same nature as God, willingly laid it all aside and became like one of us. He humbled himself to the point of sacrificing even his human rights and being crucified like a common criminal. (Philippians 2:6–8 author's translation)

Theologians call this *kenosis* or self-emptying. It clearly didn't start with Jesus' arrival on our planet but is always part of the nature of God. In Jesus it is just made crystal clear. Nor should we limit this simply to the death of Christ on the cross, central to human history though this is. God constantly self-empties, and no more so than in human suffering. The Deist view of God was impassive and distant, but that is just not true. God suffers with his creation. He suffers with us and is with us in our sufferings. He is our Comforter and our Sustainer and, as with the cross, the suffering becomes the vehicle of salvation.

This makes little sense to the dualistic mind that sees suffering only as bad luck or punishment, rather than seeing some greater purpose in it. Simply getting angry about this causes us to miss out on just about everything that really matters.

It's a pity Jesus Christ has become a swear word (or two swear words), but I suppose it does stop people forgetting his name. Remember, when you next hear it, that it means The Anointed God who Saves. Not quite what the average blasphemer has in mind, maybe, but it'll do. I imagine Jesus pricking up his ears and saying, 'Did someone just call my name?' 'Nothing. Nothing,' mumbles our embarrassed bad-mouther. 'Ah, well, just call me again when you're ready!' Jesus replies.

My point? Humility means accessibility. Jesus makes God truly accessible in a way that we can cope with. He is one who has lived like us, has been tempted like us and died worse than us. As the writer to the Hebrews put it:

We do not have a high priest who is unable to feel sympathy for our weaknesses, but we have one who has been tempted in every way, just as we are – yet he did not sin. Let us then approach God's throne of grace with confidence, so that we may receive mercy and find grace to help us in our time of need. (Hebrews 4:15–16)

Does God know what it feels like to live down here? Yes, he most certainly does! Does he still live here? By his Holy Spirit, yes. All over the world, all the time, identifying with our redemptive pain that, like his, will bring about the birth of a new creation (Romans 8:18–23).

We find out that God isn't the big scary bogeyman in the sky but is revealed in Jesus as a really nice guy that people feel comfortable with – at least, most of the time. It doesn't do to play the religious hypocrite when he's around, and if you are the devil messing up people's lives, he'll send you packing quick time. But if you are an honest human being that needs some help and understanding then he's your man.

Jesus shows us what being made in the image of God could really be like; what it means to be truly and fully human. God breathed his Spirit into the dust that made Adam, and Adam became a living person. God conceives himself in the womb of Mary by that same Holy Spirit and Jesus is born full of grace and truth. That he should sacrifice himself to right our wrongs and give us peace with God makes no sense to the two-pole thinker, but once you embrace the justice, mercy and humility of God, it makes perfect sense.

The death of Jesus was no chance event, no political miscalculation, no catastrophe. It was integral to the very shape and nature of God before anything ever was. That's why the apostle John spoke of 'the Lamb who was slain from the creation of the world' (Revelation 13:8). As we shall see later on, God was in no way caught out by the rebellion of humankind. That this would occur and that its remedy would be provided is part of the necessary nature of God and of his creation. When we really grasp this we will make sense of nearly everything that is going on, including the hard times and the difficult questions.

When I discovered the vulnerability of God I realised that I was not simply bashing my head against an immovable, impassive force, but that I could hurt God, I could give him grief, and I realised that I didn't want to. I needed his help; he could do without my resentment and rebellion. His humility allows me to come close, to live in his presence, to be again a child fascinated, curious to know. In awe, yes, but not repelled or frightened away. Maybe he and I could get to know one another better.

God is more powerful than we think, more vulnerable than we think, more present than we think. God is love, and that is drawn with beautiful grace expressed in justice, mercy and humility. It should evoke awe and wonder in our hearts.

12. God's Beauty

This first stage in our quest has largely focused on our intellectual understanding. We have touched on some of the limits of human knowledge, yet seen enough to recognise a pattern that challenges our common polarised approach to life. That still leaves us with Mystery, something that was recognised in Bible times.

> Do you think you can explain the mystery of God? Do you think you can diagram God Almighty? God is far higher than you can imagine, far deeper than you can comprehend, stretching farther than earth's horizons, far wider than the endless ocean. (Job 11:7–9 MSG)

Looking at the vastness of everything, we must surely agree – and give up. Settle instead for agnosticism, humbly acknowledging our inability to be more certain than to say, maybe.

However, before we despair, let's recognise that there are other ways of 'knowing'. For example, most of us bond into a knowing of our mothers long before we can give intellectual content to why that is so. Traditionally, the most beautiful object a man encounters is his wife's naked body on their wedding night. She may not conform to any cultural ideals of proportion, skin tone or the like but he has just experienced a much higher and wondrous kind of knowing. If you like, a revelation or an epiphany. The Song of Songs is an entire book in the Bible devoted to the mutual admiration of two lovers for each other. Then there are those transforming moments when we listen to great music or look at inspiring art.

Follow the path up from the beach to enjoy a cliff walk and gaze on the blue-lit isles and rocky bays on a bright summer's day. Take a deep breath and be transported by the beauty of the view. They say that beauty is in the eye of the beholder. This is often recited as a rather boring cliché to dismiss the importance of, or the response to, what we find beautiful. Yet although the appreciation of beauty is somewhat culturally determined by the emotionally and aesthetically immature, the most obvious fact is that humans possess this capacity universally. This really is a wonderful world, and if we miss appreciating it, it's the fault of our retrograde culture, not because beauty has disappeared.

We should not treat our capacity for beauty as lesser knowledge. It is the opposite; a higher and more complex kind of knowing and one that inspires us more than a simple analysis of how things work.

So, what happens when we consider the beauty of God?

For the average person God is alien, scary, not to say ugly. God turns up at funerals. He is the God of paedophile priests and vicious nuns. God is the religious justification for fundamentalist atrocities, the Inspirer of crimes against humanity. He appears to be associated in our minds with pain and injustice, and unwilling or unable to do anything about it. Search for the needle in the haystack and you may well prick your finger should you find it. How can you call God beautiful?

My simple response is to say that such a nasty God is not the one I experience, nor is he the one that nature and the Bible reveal as the genuine article. Most of us, including myself, find much of religion ugly and offensive, and often with good reason. So let's take a moment to say something about religion and the bad name it gives God.

You may fear that this adventure will turn you into a fundamentalist or a fanatic. There are people out there, some atheists, some Muslims, some Hindus, some Christians, some Secularists, some politically correct liberals, some racists, who express their beliefs in a particularly aggressive manner. They all have this in common: they are religious in their determination to impose their beliefs on us, often violently, always intolerantly; their faith is one of war, censorship and intimidation.

Now, my own seashore journey has taught me that love and grace are better than a punch in the face or a bullet in the back, let alone a terrorist bomb. I have no time at all for violent fundamentalism in any shape or form. Beliefs imposed by force are abusive and in my view a form of madness. People who act like this are bullies pure and simple. Morally and spiritually they have nothing worth having.

Let me say clearly that truly finding God will have the very opposite effect to this kind of fundamentalism. This is a journey of free enquiry that respects your views and at no point will I seek to intimidate you, judge you, or damn you – and for that matter neither will God. There may be challenges but it is entirely up to you whether you want to take them on or not. You are free to opt out at any time and you should feel no worse than, say, refusing to climb Mount Kilimanjaro if you have a weak heart and no head for heights. Whatever, you do not have to become a fundamentalist if you find this lost God.

Let's be honest, people are frightened by fundamentalism, and what frightens us also makes us angry. For example, many people declare that they hate the church because unthinkingly they tar it with the same brush as American fundamentalism. Or, ignoring the fact that today's British churches have some of the best child protection policies in the land, they associate them with the Irish Roman Catholic paedophile scandal. That's as silly as identifying all Muslims with terrorism, or all scientists as atheists. It's just plainly not true, but it's what we do when we are afraid.

For these and many other reasons people avoid religion and its institutions. Yet, the niggle remains. People do their best to believe without belonging. Almost everyone prays at some time or other. In spite of the prejudice in our society, there are decent Christians and Muslims and Jews and Sikhs and Buddhists and Pagans and Hindus. Many of them are good neighbours that you may know. Most people in the world still do believe in God, some of them among the most intelligent people on earth. Faith motivates vast numbers of people to give sacrificially of their time, money and energy to the relief of suffering, which is a sight better than plotting how to blow people up.

So, leaving aside the abusers of God's reputation, might he not be attractive, even beautiful, after all?

The cliché 'beauty is in the eye of the beholder' doesn't really help us here because it can be used to justify almost anything, including all the atrocities that the perpetrator may find beautiful in his own perverted eye. The serial killer may consider his actions a work of art! Yet, can we ever get beyond our own cultural norms and find universal measures of beauty? Possibly not, in any absolute sense, but there are some guidelines that may be helpful.

The first is simply our instinct to look for harmony and pattern. At its basic level it is a survival skill, helping us to make sense of our environment. But it is more than that. The artist William Hogarth noted the line of beauty; a serpentine, harmonious curve that just seems to work, like the golden mean of 1:1.62 in architecture. This line also follows our familiar wave form and is much used by artists because of its evident beauty, liveliness and harmony. Its most obvious manifestation is the classic hourglass curve of the female figure, but it may be used equally in landscape, in still life or any other artistic work. As we follow our shoreline, especially in Britain, we may note that it consists of many sweeping inlets and bays, but the same principle is also revealed in winding rivers, the rise and fall of mountain ranges and meandering pathways, that so please the eye.

Many mathematicians are entranced by the beautiful symmetry and elegance of their equations and it is something that goes beyond logic. As Stephen Hawking once asked: 'What is it that breathes fire into the equations and makes a universe for them to describe?'[8] I would probably say, 'Who', but that's by the by.

To rule out a stunning creative Mind behind it all is quite arbitrary. Even if our theories of the origins of the universe prove true, they are quite remarkable in the way that they have produced this vast cosmos, let alone people like us who can contemplate it. It is perfectly reasonable to attribute this to an elegant scientific and mathematical Source, a Genius, a beautiful Mind who should be admired and possibly worshipped.

The helical form that I have suggested as the 'shape of God' is intrinsically beautiful and is fundamental to so much that we find beautiful, from seashells to nebulae, and winding rivers to undulating hills. The helix is one of the ways that God reveals his own beauty and artistry, and contemplating such works of God is a legitimate way of contemplating the beauty of God himself. Anyone who moves beyond the train-spotting version of star-gazing may find themselves doing precisely that. Exploring the rhythms of the universe can lead into the flow of God's heart and mind. Look for the pattern and you will discover God's fingerprints.

One of the problems we humans have is that if we don't take this route we are apt to lapse into idol worship instead. Even secularists, let alone the superstitious, may adopt a thoroughly unscientific false piety when describing the natural world. The apostle Paul contends:

For since the creation of the world God's invisible qualities – his eternal power and divine nature – have been clearly seen, being understood from what has been made, so that people are without excuse. For although they knew God, they neither glorified him as God nor gave thanks to him, but their thinking became futile and their foolish hearts were darkened. Although they claimed to be wise, they became fools and exchanged the glory of the immortal God for images made to look like a mortal human being and birds and animals and reptiles . . . They exchanged the truth about God for a lie, and worshipped and served created things rather than the Creator. (Romans 1:20–23, 25)

This appreciation of God as the Source, as distinct from the created world, made possible our scientific endeavour in the West. Once you desacralise nature, that is, you stop treating it as magical or infused with animalistic spirits that you need either to placate or worship, it becomes possible to investigate it without blasphemy. The tree, the mountain, the river, is just that – maybe beautiful but certainly not divine. You are safe to explore! Indeed, it is God himself who invites us into the scientific process and he takes delight in us uncovering his secrets, just as parents take pleasure in setting up a treasure hunt for their children and watching their progress in discovering the hidden sweets and toys.

We should keep our categories clear. Creation is beautiful; God is beautiful – but Creation is not God, and God is not Creation.

Maybe we cannot yet sense what others sense. Does that mean they are self-deluded? I have difficulties hearing certain frequencies; as a result I sometimes cannot hear what others can. All I get is a high frequency whistle. Yet I would be a fool to ignore my friends when they tell me my mobile phone is ringing just because I can't hear it. It makes sense to believe their experience and answer the thing.

So, if you cannot at this moment sense either the existence of God or the beauty of God, don't worry. But don't give up either. Far more intelligent people than us have in the past contemplated the beauty of God and at times have struggled. Yet they got there, often expressing that beauty in artistic, musical and written form which today is universally recognised by educated and uneducated people alike as inspired and inspiring work of genius.

Any artist will tell you that we need to open our eyes and see what is actually present, to perceive beauty in the commonplace, and so on and so forth, but actually it is our minds that need to be opened to the broader possibilities of God. The transcendent 'Ah!', or even the 'Aha!', is not foolish or sentimental; it is an essential part of being human, and is anything but stupid or fanciful.

Part of our problem is that we have lost the art of stillness, quietude and contemplation. Thanks to the ubiquitous smartphone we have largely lost contact with our immediate environment and with one another, making us one of the most 'connected' but lonely and alienated societies ever to have existed.

'Be still and know that I am God' is ancient advice for getting in touch with ourselves and with the divine. This does not require a lengthy pilgrimage or heroic self-denial, but it does mean spending a bit of time with the phone off, away from the bustle of competing interests. Perhaps you can sit on a park bench, by the sea. Or enter a cathedral, or sit under the stars, or in a decent art gallery, museum or library. If like me you don't sit still easily, then walk in the woods or along a nature trail, or beach front. Anything that takes us away from the distracting demands of everyday life. It doesn't take a lot of time, but it does need time to listen to more subtle sounds, to see what we usually miss. You will be amazed how your perceptions grow. As you develop this habit you might begin to sense something deeper; what we call the presence of God.

The process of discovering inner peace may well open us up to another lost reality: the idea of moral and spiritual beauty.

Moral Beauty

Our modern-day reaction against rigid moral law and religious rituals and regulations makes it difficult to appreciate the beauty of God expressed through his laws. Yet past generations delighted in the idea of moral perfection; they celebrated the notion of God's holiness, equating it with the beauty of the laws of nature and with the finest craftsmanship. In a post-truth world of moral corruption, political spin and financial double-dealing there is something incredibly attractive about a pure, essential goodness (for that is what lies behind the idea of holiness). God is good; truly, utterly, splendidly so. He is perfect, and he is worthy of our admiration.

Yet that goodness doesn't find its highest expression in an idealised stained glass window of geometric perfection. Instead, it is found in Jesus, of whom the apostle John could write,

> And Christ became a human being and lived here on earth among us and was full of loving forgiveness and truth. And some of us have seen his glory – the glory of the only Son of the heavenly Father! (John 1:14 TLB)

Jesus was simply the most beautiful man who ever lived, a living work of art that provoked in equal measure awe and wonder, and outrage and envy.

The eyewitnesses saw him as God incarnate; a man without sin who lived among the most assiduous sin-hunters in the world; the unblemished man who would willingly sacrifice himself for all of us. He is a man who loved men and women but never leered at them; someone who never lied or cheated or played the hypocrite. This is the Jesus who went about doing good, healing, restoring, forgiving, inspiring, revealing what God was really like to a world full of needy people.

Jesus was no ascetic killjoy; you would find him in the tavern enjoying good company and a well-earned pint; he would be cracking jokes with children and blessing families, drawing our eyes to the richness of God's providential blessings as he shared good food with friends and neighbours. Little wonder it was prophesied about him: 'You are the most excellent of men and your lips have been anointed with grace, since God has blessed you for ever' (Psalm 45:2).

Worship, corporate and private, is an integral part of the Christian faith. It encompasses the whole gamut of human emotion and artistic expression. Its forms range from quiet meditation to vibrant celebration; it expresses culture but it also shapes culture. It never compels but it is compelling. So, why worship? Why celebrate? Why write the most enduring poetry and songs? Why paint the Sistine Chapel? Why craft the Lindisfarne Gospels? Why compose the *Messiah*? Why build iconic cathedrals? Certainly not to earn God's favour. Christians worship out of gratitude and appreciation, not as a way of paying for their ticket to heaven. It is because they admire the genius, the scientific beauty, the artistic glory, the moral perfection of God and all his works and feel it is worth at least a round of applause! As Psalm 146 in the Bible song book puts it: 'Praise the LORD, O my soul. I will praise the LORD all my life; I will sing praise to my God as long as I live.'

No surprise then that the Christian faith is such a major inspiration for art. This is why so many artists, writers and musicians find their spiritual home in church. True art is both an expression of beauty and a prophetic call to challenge the status quo – and that is what the church should be about: celebration and confrontation. Far from being a haven for the twee, safe or reactionary, replete with crosses and doves, Christian-inspired art will find beauty in strange places, and expose corruption beneath pretty veneers. It will face honestly the problem of suffering and evil but it will also offer redemption and hope. And that is the beauty of God in action.

Death

13. The Elephant in the Room

The previous chapter may have made you angry. If so, you have my sympathy because by itself it could sound like a fairy story where nothing goes wrong. Yet we know that life is full of troubles and is hard for the majority of us. I have spoken with millionaires and with paupers and it is obvious that neither wealth nor poverty brings happiness. Adversity may take many forms but it is inescapable. For this reason, no view of God can avoid the reality of suffering and pain. For every beautiful sunset over the sea there is a raging hurricane, a devastating earthquake, a lightning strike and a tsunami in paradise.

This part of our journey may seem like the 'death' phase in the cycle. A bit uncomfortable but necessary if we are to experience the 'resurrection' phase. So press on in hope if you do find this difficult!

The elephant in the room is the unpleasant fact of human pain and suffering that we try to avoid talking about. Our success-driven, youth-obsessed society prefers not to notice the deformed, the mentally ill, the bereaved, the anguished, the destitute. The fantasy world of the advertising industry has little place for grief. Even our CVs must be wholly positive. Yet pain and suffering are realities and it's no use pretending otherwise. There arose a sect in the nineteenth century that called themselves Christian Scientists, but the sect was neither Christian nor scientific. One of its tenets was that pain is an illusion. I beg to differ; there is no illusion about the pain when I hit my thumb with a hammer. Spiritualising and mystifying pain does not take away its reality for ordinary sane people. Pain hurts!

Imagine you are on a sandy beach on a warm sunny day. Lots of people are sunning themselves, splashing about in the water, building sand castles, reading, supping drinks. Suddenly, there's a commotion. An ambulance helicopter is landing on the low cliff top by the lifeguard station and cafe. You hurry to join others who gather to see what's going on. There is a sense of foreboding in the air, a coldness, though the sky is cloudless. You see two lifeguards struggling at the water's edge as they drag a man ashore. He is unconscious and his body is purple coloured. His wife and kids are distraught. Everyone is solemn in the way that you are if you pass a bad motorway crash. Sober reality hits home.

We don't know if this man is dead or can be saved. We rightly surmise that he became caught in the undertow of a rip tide and tried to fight it until he was exhausted. In theory, he should have gone with the tide until its force was spent. Easier said than done. Another holiday tragedy. Ruined lives, broken dreams. It happens all the time.

Why, Why, Why?

We live in a contradictory world of great beauty and simultaneously of great horror. It is a world of joyful births and of tragic stillbirths, of perfect babies and of miscarriages and deformities, of bright hopes and cot deaths – and that's only the beginning. Life is hard, even in the pampered West where, as the poet put it, 'all our joys are touched by pain'. For people in other parts of the world this paradox is written much larger. To be human is to suffer.

It's time to face the issue of pain and suffering in the light of a God who is supposed to be good and loving, and all powerful.

Is this the world that a good and beautiful God would create? If he did then how did he lose control? To be personal, why did my mum lose a lower limb to gangrene when she was 18 years of age? Why did my young fiancée contract type 1 diabetes just months before we married? Why were two of our children born with congenital deformities? Why did one of them nearly die in a road accident? And we are supposed to be on God's side, for goodness' sake! Is all this necessary, for some reason unavoidable? Or are we just unfortunate? Is God allowing it, or causing it? Or is this the devil's work that God can't or won't stop?

I think of dear friends of mine who have given birth to hopelessly deformed children that have needed a lifetime of care. Accidents in later life can be blamed on someone, but congenital faults can only be blamed on bad genes or bad luck, a bad devil, or a bad god. Why did he allow this? Did he cause it because of some sin of the parents? What kind of God is that? These questions don't go away with glib platitudes. In short, why do the innocent suffer?

I suppose it's easy for atheists. If there is no God, no ultimate cause, if existence is nothing more than chance, or even impersonal determinism, then there is nothing much to say. Life has no meaning beyond genetic survival, maybe based on the dubious notion of the 'selfish gene'. Right and wrong are relative and negotiable, usually in favour of the powerful, but that's how it goes. Pain and suffering have no meaning, so there is no value in asking why bad things happen. You just happened to be in the wrong place at the wrong time and took a random bullet. Bad luck! The world will carry on until its ultimate pointless heat-death at the end of time, or sooner.

In reality most atheists are neither so unfeeling nor uncaring. Reducing risk, repairing the damage, protecting the weak, improving the lot of the vulnerable, are perfectly defensible without invoking God. Evolution stands its best chance when we have a well-cared-for humanitarian society. The survival of the fittest is replaced by the survival of the most cooperative, the most symbiotic. At least, if I were an atheist that would be my enlightened choice.

However, I believe in a good God, a beautiful God, and, along with the vast majority of the human race, when I face suffering I must confront the question 'why' and come up with some reasonable answers. Presumably you are still reading this book for the same reason.

Guilty or Not?

Let's begin by addressing a common misunderstanding. Is it all your fault? Are you to blame? Counsellors and psychologists tell us that guilt is the number-one cause of mental distress and depression in our society.

One of my daughters has a severely deformed spine. One day I went to the osteopath for a routine bit of spine cracking of my own. He told me casually that I had a slight curve to my spine, nothing serious and nothing unusual. But I sat in the car park afterwards and wept thinking that my daughter's suffering was all my fault.

It is so easy to draw these false conclusions. We can blame ourselves, simply because in a cause-and-effect, contingent world we want to find a cause; but that kind of guilt feeling is entirely misplaced unless it can be specifically defined in cause-and-effect terms.

My personal example demonstrates how ridiculous this line of guilt is. 'If only my wife and I hadn't married. If only we had made love five minutes later, or on another day!' Similarly, people say, 'If only I had been there this would never have happened.' 'If only we hadn't stopped at the garage.' The list is endless.

In truth, we have almost no control over the 'if onlys' of life. Stuff happens and it's no use blaming ourselves for it. This is just false, or idiopathic, guilt. Typically, false guilt is indefinable; we have only the vaguest idea of what we may have done wrong, and there's nothing we can do to put it to rights. All we can do is torture ourselves unnecessarily. That kind of guilt should be rejected out of hand.

It's easy to tell the difference between true guilt and false guilt. True guilt is specific action known to be wrong by the perpetrator. It has the form of a wilful act against the state, against a person or persons, against oneself, or against God. The action that caused the guilt is what we may call sin, or wrongdoing. We can acknowledge it and put it to rights, or at least take the consequences for it. False guilt offers us no such remedy.

Now, the father who drove angrily and had an accident that killed or maimed his children has good reason to feel guilty. The promiscuous young woman who contracts chlamydia and becomes sterile as a result may rightly regret the unwanted consequence of her high-risk lifestyle. Properly convicted criminals should feel guilt and regret for their crimes. If you have smoked 60 a day for the past twenty years and you contract emphysema or lung cancer, then you know 'what you have done to deserve this'. You took your chance and you lost. We live in a contingent universe thanks to the consistency of God's just laws of nature. Known abuse of those laws carries built-in consequences. There is no real mystery about why you are ill. In a real sense you brought it on yourself.

However, we should always reject the generalised feeling of guilt that has no specific connection with suffering.

Especially, ill health or misfortune must not be taken as evidence of evil deeds on our part. The ancient book of Job addresses this issue. Job famously suffered the loss of work, wealth, children and health. As far as he could tell he had done nothing wrong. His friends, the so-called Job's comforters, thought otherwise, and Job rightly protests at their mistaken logic and their failure to empathise with what he was enduring. His sufferings had nothing to do with any secret sin or fault on his part. We, likewise, would do well not to pursue that path.

Besides, if there were any connection between adversity and evildoing then surely Adolph Hitler should have had very bad health indeed. Likewise, Stalin, and Pol Pot, and so on. The Bible is very honest about this. The wicked seem often to prosper at the expense of good people. Wealth and righteousness seldom go together. As for whether those upon whom disasters fall are more evil than the rest of us, well, Jesus refuted that absolutely. 'The sun rises and the rain falls on the just and the unjust alike,' he says (see Matthew 5:45). When questioned about the victims of a natural disaster and of a political atrocity, he declared that those people were no better or worse than his hearers, and his hearers had better watch out if they thought their lack of suffering meant they were morally superior. They most certainly were not!

Most people are good-hearted and caring, especially for their families and friends and often for many others in their communities and beyond. Witness the coming together and the spiritual unity of good people in the aftermath of terrorist attacks; and the massive sums of money that people give to charity to relieve poverty and famine and disaster. The last thing people should feel, either as innocent victims or as those who go to their aid, is misplaced guilt. My understanding of God as Jesus revealed him is that, whatever the mysteries of providence, he is right there with us in the suffering, offering comfort, compassion and care through our actions and by his Spirit. He is not judging us, so we should not blame ourselves for what was not our doing.

14. Human Violence

If the source of suffering is not directly to be found in the victim's specific moral failure then we must look elsewhere.

In general terms we don't have to look very far. Imagine our beautiful beach begins to smell sour. We have just encountered an unfiltered sewage outflow pipe from which trickles industrial waste and worse. It's not very pleasant and you would be unwise to swim in the waters. The most common cause of adversity, the chief generators of suffering and pain, environmental disasters and the like, are humans themselves.

Think of all the road accidents caused by carelessness, impatience and incompetence. Consider the epidemic levels of sexually transmitted infections brought on by promiscuity. Yes, I know it's not popular to say so, but it's true. Add to that our addictions to excess alcohol, drug abuse, smoking, overeating. We have, with these things alone, accounted for most of the NHS budget!

Then think about wars. The twentieth century was the most barbaric in human history and more people were killed and maimed by secular and atheistic states in those years than all those who suffered during the religious wars of all centuries previously. I'm not excusing religion, I don't much like religion, but secular aggression, greed and hatred is far and away the biggest cause of human violence. We should not be put off our quest by dishonest suggestions that religion is the root cause of war. It's just not true. In spite of the many benefits of modern technology, that same technology has also allowed us to produce weapons of mass destruction. We have industrialised death and constructed a production line in human corpses. We have turned killing into an industry. Worse, we have detached ourselves; we are bystanders to horror, watching atrocious violence on our TV screens with more indifference than the average porn addict who at least knows what he wants from his viewing.

That detachment easily removes our personal responsibility. Waging war becomes another game for a geek with a joystick 20,000 miles away from the shattered limbs and splattered blood, the writhing pain and screaming agony, caused by the click of his button. There can be no glory in these kind of wars; no heroes among those just following orders from a distance. Monstrous evil is performed by banal functionaries; it is the radical depletion of good where morality and ethics are neutralised by obedience in following orders. Nowadays, we should fear the avid law keeper as much as the law breaker.

It is war that causes most of the famines in the modern world, dispossessing people, destroying crops, poisoning the soil, depriving generations of people of hope and a future. We might add the consequences of environmental pollution brought about by exploitative multinationals and governments who think nothing of ruining the health of native populations if it will make them a quick buck. This is to say nothing of slave labour, deprivation of ancestral lands, all brought about by our desire for a cheap throwaway society.

Even when it comes to natural disasters we humans must shoulder much of the blame. Whatever we make of climate change it is likely that we play a part in the cause because of our untrammelled exploitation of the earth's resources. Even our droughts and our flash floods and mud slides owe much to aggressive deforestation. Some pundits even speculate that the earthquakes and tsunamis brought about by tectonic plate shifts are the consequence of underground nuclear testing. Launch a massive pressure ripple deep underground and who knows what we might have unleashed.

None of this will account for the catastrophes that took place before the industrial age, of course. Back then people attributed disasters to the wrath of God or gods and usually sought a moral or spiritual reason. Well, maybe, but it is seldom that simple or immediate. The narrow view of decadence and disaster might seem to fit Pompeii, but not Mount St Helena. If the mills of God are turning then they do so slowly and less directly. Searching for connections between environmental catastrophes and morally corrupt societies is seldom satisfactory and we might use our energies more profitably in helping the victims.

In spite of all this, most people are decent, hard-working and caring folk who are doing their best. I have seldom come across truly evil people, by which I mean those who consciously and maliciously perpetrate harm on others. The majority of us make mistakes, fall short of our own standards, and commit minor misdemeanours from time to time, but mostly we are the victims of other people's wrongdoing. What I mean is, there's a world of difference between the albeit imperfect young people attending a pop concert in Manchester and the sheer wickedness of the terrorist bomber.

Hypocrisy

I have just used the word evil and a very unpopular one it is today, almost as unpopular as the word sin. Some object to it because they believe evil is in the eye of the beholder. 9/11 was evil, but not the bombing of Baghdad, for example. But that view can equally be reversed, depending on which side you are on.

Furthermore, we do not consider ourselves evil, so we resent the implication that we might be. Our reactions to such suggestions are understandable. 'How dare you! How would you know? Have you been stalking me? Are you accusing me of being a paedophile, a rapist, a drug dealer, or a murderer? Do you think I'm gay? Who asked you, anyway? Do you get some perverse pleasure out of spreading this misery? I may not be perfect but I'm as good as the next man. I live and let live and do my best to treat people decently. They leave me alone; I leave them alone. And, yes, I do give to charity, and I recycle my rubbish, before you ask. Bloody hypocrite!'

The danger with this self-righteous opinion of ourselves is that it detaches us from the problem. We develop a tabloid view of society. Recently, the evil monsters were the celebrity paedophiles. Before that it was crooked MPs and bent coppers. If not them then militant Muslim clerics, or industrial fat cats, or bankers. Currently, in post-Brexit Britain, it appears to be all foreigners! There is always someone else to blame. The problem is that in scapegoating others, we excuse ourselves of our own misdemeanours and attitudes.

Whatever the supposed reasons for our problems they lie elsewhere than blaming people on the basis of unfounded rumour, or stereotyping them. 'The only good (scapegoat of your choice) is a dead (scapegoat of your choice)' mentality is frankly insane, and only makes matters worse.

For most of us, blaming others is a cop-out. We are all hypocrites when it comes to what we are like on the inside. Given enough power and money, we might behave with equal arrogance, we might indulge our appetites and grow indifferent to abusing others in the process. The monsters in our society are people like us, and who is to say that we might not behave like them given the right conditions? The arrogant mob can make criminals of us all.

In his science fiction novel *That Hideous Strength* C.S. Lewis speaks of the peer pressure of the senior board room that perverts the newly arrived innocent, that encourages the abuse of privilege because 'you are now one of us', that mocks those who don't participate as being intellectually inferior, that threatens social ostracism. If you want to get on then you must become like us.

That peer pressure applies just as much to a sex and booze stag night in Prague, accepting the dodgy freebies in business, fiddling expense claims, filching from the building site or factory, happy slapping, binge drinking, even malicious gossip. Everybody does it, and if you don't, you get the rest of us in trouble. Witness the massive amount of shoplifting, the perceived need for security cameras at every turn. The terrible truth about the celebrity child abusers is that they could only get away with it because of a peer culture that accepted that 'this sort of thing goes on and we turn a blind eye'. Don't let anyone betray 'the talent'! Add to that the professional foul, the business lie, the local councillor's or the MP's backhander, the deal behind the deal where we 'understand one another'. Meanwhile, we are encouraged to develop our blameless, flawless persona, our mask, 'because we're worth it'. The world is full of hypocrites, and sometimes it includes ourselves!

15. A Great Fall

I think my personal Paradise, my Garden of Eden, would have to be beside the sea. It would include rocky Cornish bays and cliffs, soft sand and splendid surf. It would be south facing but protected from too much wind (a light breeze will be sufficient) and be pleasantly warm and sunny all year round. Naturally, my wife and children and grandchildren would be there, and even some of my friends. All cultivation and creativity would be fruitful, and every day a fulfilling delight. Jesus would meet up with us every day and enthral us with all the delights of creation. And we would eat wonderful food, and drink the best coffee, wine and beer imaginable.

I can but dream!

The Bible opens with the creation of just such a paradise. OK, not quite like mine but nonetheless a place of goodness and bliss – a perfect Garden of Eden in which lived two perfect people, Adam and Eve. Sadly, they disobeyed an environmental command, 'Eat from this tree and it will poison you. You will die.' The result of their transgression was ecological, social, and spiritual disaster; the garden was lost to a wilderness, their relationship grew violent and manipulative; pain became a reality. They also lost an easy personal relationship with God their Creator and so began the story of human religion to make up for it.

Whatever we make of the Genesis story, whether you consider it literal or not, isn't the prime issue. What it does do is make us face the reality of our human condition and it suggests an underlying spiritual cause to this: the assertion of our own egos and the need for an effective remedy. It also suggests a malevolence, a personification of evil sometimes called the devil or Satan, the serpent or the dragon. It even indicates that this being was created good but fell into hubris or arrogance, desiring out of envy the supreme position of equality to God. Not being granted his wishes, he then set about corrupting the planet and its inhabitants.

Do good angels exist? What about bad ones? Are there such entities, elementary spiritual forces, that we may call demons? Is there a malevolent devil behind all that is wrong? The biblical writers obviously thought so, though this was never their central theme. The ancient book of Job certainly recognises the activity of Satan with regard to Job's sufferings. Maddeningly, Satan is able to afflict poor old Job with God's, albeit limited, permission!

Anecdotal evidence abounds, both ancient and modern, for the personification of evil. I know people who have sensed a disembodied malevolent presence, have experienced frightening telekinesis, have even smelt the presence of evil. Whether this is purely subjective is, of course, a matter of opinion. It will not do to dismiss it lightly as mere superstition. Patterns of evil do sometimes emerge that are beyond the bounds of chance and probability and certainly appear to have a malign intelligence behind them. As W.H. Auden put it, 'Evil is not a by-product of circumstances. There has to be a reason why Hitler was utterly wrong.'

However, and it is a big however, even if this be true, we should not overstate the case and start looking for demons behind every lamp post. 'The devil made me do it,' is absolutely no excuse for our bad behaviour; he is introduced in the story as a tempter, but it is we who sin.

Some versions of Christian theology suggest that the Fall was absolute. Nature and human nature alike were ruined. We are totally depraved and even our apparent goodness is a cover-up for deeply corrupt natures. Any goodness in the world is only because of God's providence and we're lucky to have even that! Worse still, we are all corporately and individually guilty of Adam's original sin. Now, I have never bought into this idea, not least because logically if even our reason is corrupt then we could not think that we are corrupt without that in itself being a corrupt thought! Unless, of course, we slip in a piece of special divine revelation. But that is cheating.

Nor do I find us humans, for all our faults, to be incapable of altruistic love and goodness. I was criticised by some in America for my novel *Hallow's Deep* (originally, *A Distant Shore*) because I suggested that my central characters could be genuinely happy and in love. What's wrong with that? you may ask. Ah, because they were not Christians and were living in sin, i.e. having sex but not married. I was told that their happiness must be a delusion and it is my duty to portray it as such!

Yet I know vast numbers of people who live genuinely happy lives, even though they are 'sinners' of this kind. These people are loyal, loving, sacrificial, and often coping with difficulties that I know I could never myself handle. It would stick in my throat to suggest for one moment that all these people are fooling themselves and one another, or that their love was a satanic deception! Yes, I believe in marriage and I believe in faith but I also believe that genuine goodness can be found in people who do not necessarily have Christian faith.

The problem once more is our dualistic mindset taken to extremes. Whatever God may or may not make of it, there is a world of difference between the average sinner and the truly wicked who are motivated by malice aforethought. Sin is sin and a small sin might lead to a bigger one, but sin is not all the same either in extent or impact. It is one thing to comment on human society as a whole, as Paul does in Romans chapters 1 and 3, and find that we are a corrupted creation compared to the standard of God's law. It is quite another to make this a blanket condemnation of every individual, irrespective of the fruit of their own lives.

Between chapters 1 and 3 of Romans lies chapter 2 where Paul identifies non-Jewish individuals declaring, 'Some people live for

God's glory, for honour, and for life that cannot be destroyed. They live for those things by always continuing to do good. God will give eternal life to them' (Romans 2:7 ERV). It takes humility to live for others than ourselves and that creates once more the triangle: that triad of justice, mercy and humility, which turns a straight line into a zone of grace and that pleases God. It would be right out of context to limit those people to card-carrying church members. Indeed, I will go further. The closer we approach humility of spirit and action, the closer we come to Jesus and eternal life, whatever our religion. The more arrogant we become the closer we move towards the devil.

This will upset some church attenders and theologians because their security is found in their formulae and in conformity to their rules of belonging. These people will accuse me of minimising sin, of suggesting salvation by works; they will amass proof texts lifted out of context and quote their mantras. In a previous age they would probably burn me at the stake. Yet I contend that this not-so-subtle theology of exclusion is precisely why there are so many people who believe in God, pray for help and forgiveness and God's presence, even believe in Jesus, but do not belong to a church.

Ask them, as I have, and you will find that they were stumbled by a priggish self-righteousness, a Pharisaism that filters the select elect at the door of their temple according to whether they are deemed fit enough. They have felt rejected by those whom the apostle James questions, 'Have you not discriminated among yourselves and become judges with evil thoughts?' (James 2:4). They would, of course, bar Jesus in the name of Jesus!

Dear fellow believers, when will we get it into our silly heads that 'the love of God is broader than the measure of man's mind, and the heart of the Eternal is most wonderfully kind'? It's not about theological check lists but about people whose hearts are in the right place; people who know him even though they don't know his name. Karl Rahner speaks of those whose lives are a prayer but who don't think they are praying because they haven't learned the right words. The label on the heart is far more important than the label on the door.

We dare not limit God's saving grace, let alone his common grace. In the midst of all the suffering and evil, God still bestows kindness on the human race. This includes not only the providential blessings of food and water and the like, but also genuine human love and sacrifice, the relief of poverty, helping the needy for no reason other than human compassion and care.

The image may be marred but it is not totally ruined. We are magnificent ruins and still bear traces of the glory that once was ours. That is why the poet wrote:

> You made humans just a little lower than angels; you crowned us with splendour; you gave us authority and put us in charge of all you have made. (Psalm 8:5–6 author's translation)

Redemption is still possible. There may be an elephant in the room but it doesn't necessarily fill every square centimetre of available space!

All this still begs the question: given the thesis that there is a good God, a beautiful Creator God, who is helical in essential nature and is revealed as Father, Son and Holy Spirit; given that this planet and the humans who dwell here are seriously damaged; given even that there might be a sinister malevolence behind it all, why the hell doesn't God put it all to rights? Why doesn't he stop the pain? Why did God allow this Fall?

Even granted that humans are responsible for most of the evils in the world, why does God not intervene, particularly on behalf of the innocent? Supposing for one moment that we were to blame the devil for it all, which I certainly do not, then why doesn't God blast him to smithereens? Or is the devil as strong as God? Do we actually live in a yin-yang world where good and evil are equally opposed and where that balance is necessary for existence? Have we shifted from being a Western bipolar society to becoming an Eastern one? Or does our three-fold way offer another explanation?

16. The Only Possible Universe

The seashore presents us with some weird creatures, doesn't it? Crabs, lobsters, shrimps; limpets, cockles, mussels, oysters; starfish, jellyfish, crayfish. What interests us is that these creatures do not live in an either/or environment, but a both/and one. They are remarkably adapted to the only world they experience – one that is decidedly wave form and rhythmical. Part of the challenge for ourselves is to look at reality through better lenses and adapt to what actually is rather than what our culture has taught us.

It is very tempting to apportion blame for all the ills of the world, but that option neither solves the problem nor does it get us very far. Even in the case of human criminality trying to make the punishment fit the crime proves to be immensely complex. If justice is done and seen to be done we may feel vindicated, satisfied, as well we should and might, but history still happened. As the years roll by, nothing brings back our world before the crime was committed.

Perhaps we blame God for all that goes wrong. OK, but what has that actually achieved? It probably makes us feel a little more self-righteous, i.e. I'm not as guilty as God! With the corollary: if there's a judgement day then it should be God in the dock, not me. That still leaves us trying to quantify evil, to put it on a scale. So why not blame it all on the devil? But we're still left with the problem of why a good God would create a bad devil and a messed up world. There is another way, a third option. Applying ternary (three pole) thinking, there is a possibility that makes better sense of reality. It's not an altogether comfortable one but it's this: given the nature of God this is the only possible universe that he could have created.

We can look at this as a virtuous golden circle, i.e. if the shape of God is helical then so must be the universe; and if the universe is helical then so must God be, too. It follows that this life, death, resurrection universe is the only possible one. It will not satisfy everyone because it relies on accepting a coherence between creation and revelation, between what we see in nature, what we read in the Bible and what we perceive in our own psyches. But I maintain that this is a reasonable coherence.

We have to accept the reality of our given world. However much it might be fun to speculate on other possibilities – non-carbon-based life forms like trolls and robots, pluriverses, and the like – we are concerned to find something that works at the street level of our own existence. We can only know what is, not what might have been. To all intents and purposes this is the only universe we've got or could actually experience.

Furthermore, because God is good, he would never create an evil universe, and nor could he. He would also create the best that is possible, given his own nature and his power to do what he wills. The genius of God would rule out all other lesser possibilities. Again, what we have is the best possible, given that his intent was to create people who would love him freely and also receive his love freely.

Does this set limits on God? Yes, it does! For those who are going to get uppity at this point let me remind you that the Bible tells us that God cannot deny himself, that is, he cannot act contrary to who he is. God is love; God is good; God is pure. He cannot author evil; he cannot hate by nature; he cannot be the devil. He is who he is, and he will always act according to that nature, no more, no less.

All acts of creation require decisions to include and decisions to exclude. Those decisions spring from who we are and what we wish to achieve. We do this imperfectly. God gets it exactly right, which is why I say again that what we have is the only possible universe.

Does this matter? Yes, because at some point in life, and that may well be during a testing time, we have to accept the reality of our world if we are to make any further progress in our life's journey. We have to leave behind our 'if onlys' and begin to deal with what is, not what might have been. Wishful thinking must give way to action, and the starting point is to recognise that this is the only possible universe because it is the one that God did, in fact, make.

The Rhythm of Life

Now if love is just, and humble, and merciful then those factors will determine the shape of the universe, the helical life, death and resurrection pattern. What then will this mean?

First, that rhythm, cycles of life and death and renewed life will be fundamental to creation. This we have already noted clearly enough and we are on solid ground with it. It seems not to present problems. Seed time, harvest and winter. Waking, sleeping, waking. The rain cycle. Sound waves, the electromagnetic spectrum. We humans are well adapted to these processes and know how to use them to our advantage.

Those rhythms were present even in the perfect Garden of Eden, for we should not imagine Adam and Eve in static medieval poses standing among strategically placed bushes hiding their naughty bits. They worked; they spoke; they made love; they slept; they ate. All this requires rhythm, the rise, the fall, the rising again. There is even an element of dying, otherwise how else could Adam and Eve eat? When we ingest food our bodies strip out the DNA and incorporate it into our own. This is the process we call digestion. The seeds in Eden must fall into the ground and die to produce fresh crops. It doesn't even necessarily rule out the possibility of carnivorous animals (though Adam and Eve were vegetarians themselves). That may be taking it too far because the renewed creation suggests that the lion lays down with the lamb rather than laying the table to devour the lamb!

That's the given of the created physical world. Let's turn now to human society, the cosmos as in civilisation. Ezekiel had a vision of what can best be described as a differential gearbox; wheels within wheels that allow the vehicle to change direction at right angles. Supposing there are wheels, big wheels, in which our smaller wheels turn? I am thinking of the great cycles of history, the rise and fall of nations and empires, the global economic booms and recessions, the golden ages and the barbarian ages. Why should these not be inevitably what God would build in because they are essentially according to his nature and purpose?

Let's take this a step further. Why should not a God of love elect for a world in which the Fall would take place because that was the only way that he could achieve the end goal of people who would freely love him and achieve the very best possible life? It used to be said, somewhat unkindly to the feline population I always thought, that there is more than one way to skin a cat. Sometimes there is only one way, even if it proves to be a difficult one. Maybe we will have to trust the greater wisdom of God in this matter; perhaps reach that stage where the apostle Paul could write, 'we know that all that happens to us is working for our good if we love God and are fitting into his plans' (Romans 8:28 TLB).

That this includes the pattern of a Fall, suffering, and redemption is then for us a fact of life that we might challenge, baulk at, regret, but in the final analysis it is what we have to live with. How to do so constructively, particularly in our difficult times, is the theme of a later chapter.

Falling Upwards

Such a creation that requires a necessary Fall would not catch God out, nor would it make him morally responsible for evil, since it is the only way that the goal of love could be fulfilled. That God should create a world in which the possibility of evil – that is, of his sentient creations of angels and men rebelling, and even of knowing that they would – does not make him culpable since it is just a given of his own existence.

Love must include choice and that must be fair and free. If you offer me two poisoned chalices to drink from then you have not given me choice any more than if you gave me a choice of two glasses of the finest wine. I know which I would prefer, but I could never grow up unless I was faced with genuine alternatives. I could never truly love unless I have the option not to love. Any other way would be illusory. The death element, the option of evil, even the devil himself, must be there if I am to choose the good and to have life.

Theoretically, even God could do evil because he 'knows', that is, he is aware of that choice between good and evil, but he being love, being good, being truly free, only ever chooses the good. 'When tempted, no one should say, "God is tempting me." For God cannot be tempted by evil, nor does he tempt anyone; but each person is tempted when they are dragged away by their own evil desire and enticed' (James 1:13–14).

This may help answer the question, 'Where does evil come from?' Evil is not an entity, it is an absence; it is the lack of love. We give too much credence to evil and to darkness. As a novelist I know that it is easier to portray evil than it is to express convincing goodness. Anyone can imagine monsters. That says more about our perceptions of life than about the reality. Our news programmes are actually bad news programmes. Good news doesn't sell!

Evil is simply the negation of love and it can be cancelled by restoring love. If you don't like the darkness simply turn the light on. This is why it is a mistake to suggest that God and the devil, or good and evil are somehow equally polarised. There really is no comparison between the absence of good and the good itself. Some things are a matter of choice. We'll keep that thought in mind for later.

The classic Genesis story of the Fall of man was all about choice. We are presented with two fruit trees. One tree offered eternal life, an unbroken intimate relationship with God with all the unsullied delight of children let loose in a cosmic playground to learn and discover, to create and rejoice in God's creative genius. The other tree offered only conflict, moral dilemma and death. Knowing good and evil meant living with self-contradiction and social alienation. The universe would grow hostile, knowledge hard to come by and easily abused, religion a substitute for a close relationship with God. There would be no easy access to the tree of life. Adam and Eve were driven from the Garden and like us would die. They, like us, would have to make a journey, a journey from life, through death, to resurrection. In the process they might grow up into a maturity never possible in the Garden.

This has led some to call this the happy Fall, since God in his sovereignty had this necessarily in mind from the beginning, because it is the only way that we might find the true freedom of spiritual adulthood. John Milton expresses it thus in *Paradise Lost*:

> O goodness infinite, goodness immense!
> That all this good of evil shall produce,
> And evil turn to good; more wonderful
> Than that by which creation first brought forth
> Light out of darkness![9]

'A God who can take all evil, even the mistakes and sins of a penitent child of God, and by the alchemy of His divine grace so transform them that they boomerang against Satan, enhance the character of the Saint, and redound to the glory of God, is worthy of unceasing praise.'[10]

Is it possible to fall upwards? Well, yes, it is. Remember the helical pattern – a life, death, resurrection. That which never dies can never experience resurrection, but 'dying' is the threshold to transformation. Embrace the principle and our spirits circle ever upwards like ascending birds.

17. Negating Love

Even if we accept the possibility of the Fall, perhaps going so far as to say it is somehow necessary in the mysterious purpose of God, surely we cannot call this evil good? Isn't this just confusing the issue? Are we not obliged to see life as good versus evil rather than seeing good coming out of evil? You don't redeem cancer, you kill it. You don't offer therapy to the child abusers, you bang them up for life. You don't accommodate drug dealers, you smash their businesses. Surely God, any god worth calling by that name, cannot be involved in Hitler's death camps or the Soviet gulags?

Any so-called big-picture purpose surely leaves God ruthlessly pursuing his plan while we writhe and scream down here with some nebulous 'pie in the sky' hope of everlasting life – if that even exists – if only we can survive the pain without going mad. Such a God is still the absent landlord of Deism. In fact, it might be better if he were because then we wouldn't waste our time shouting at him.

Furthermore, am I not trivialising evil by making it the mere absence of love?

To answer this charge we will have to appreciate just how good and powerful love is, how utterly all-consuming is the sacrificial drive that will do anything for the good of the beloved, how Godlike and at the same time normal this is meant to be. We will have to imagine a universe where love prevails at all times. Only then can we recognise the enormity of negating such love.

I have said 'just' the absence of love, but the malevolence

involved in negating love is appalling and the consequences even worse. We pass a mother sitting on a rock, about to breast feed her baby. The trusting infant reaches out in innocence for its mother's breast. To our horror the mother reaches for a club hammer and smashes it into her baby's face, laughing as she does so. We are shocked, appalled by the atrocity. Vividly, we have just witnessed the negation of love.

Somewhat shaken, we must consider further what it means to negate love. Nature, as we know, abhors a vacuum and the negation of love in our lives, or in our societies, or even among our nations, means replacing it with self love. Our egos become the only motive for our existence. It means we regress to two-and-a-half-year-olds in the playroom where we snatch toys, hit our sister on the head with a doll, throw tantrums, lie and cheat and steal. To negate love is to arrest and reverse our growth to moral and spiritual maturity; it is to oppose the process that God has instituted for our full humanity.

It is anti-evolutionary; for we must not see evolution simply in biological terms. What would be the point of creatures more developed than us biologically – say, having that third hand which would be so useful when you are trying to tie a parcel – if they did not have a better morality and social cohesion than us? We may theorise about the next stage of evolution but it will never occur unless we can grow up morally and spiritually, simply because intellectual or physical improvement will be blocked by our destructive egotism. Already, we are capable of annihilating ourselves; we don't want to become more capable!

To negate love is to justify our own interests no matter what suffering it causes to others, be that war, economic ruin, genocide, torture. It is to act contrary to the golden rule that we should do to others as we would do for ourselves. Ultimately, it is to create hell.

Now before we mild-mannered civilised people absolve ourselves from responsibility, let me remind us that most evils are committed not by fiends but by people in smart business suits making boardroom decisions in the name of whatever, at the cost of other people's well-being. It's when we reject win-win in favour of hostile, asset-stripping takeovers with little regard for job losses. It's when for the sake of fame and profit, local councillors agree planning orders that ruin the environment. It's when government ministers secure lucrative trade deals at the price of economic slavery. It's the suited bankers who fund wars, the investors in commodities and futures who ruin farmers and peasants for their own greed.

It comes nearer home, too, in destructive marriages ruined by self-interest, in schools where bad teachers rule by sarcasm (by the way, sarcasm means literally to tear the flesh like dogs), in sexual exploitation for our egocentric gratification. It means dominating and intimidating others around us. Recently we watched a rerun of the TV sitcom *Keeping Up Appearances*. The humour centres on the pretensions of a would-be middle-class lady named Hyacinth Bucket (must be pronounced Bouquet) and the hapless cast of relatives and neighbours kept wholly in thrall to her obsession with decency and reputation. Her well-meaning obsession with standards as opposed to love makes this well-dressed suburban lady the epitome of evil!

For younger readers, you might recognise the rule-keeping, rule-imposing horror of J.K. Rowling's Dolores Umbridge, the Hogwarts Inquisitor who tortures Harry Potter in the name of education and social conformity. She is one of the most evil characters in the series because she imposes law in place of love to suit her own ambitions.

Devilish Temptation

Satan's seduction of Eve had nothing to do with sex as is popularly supposed; it was about the rejection of normative sacrificial love in favour of self-love – a self-love that would and has grown to monstrous proportions. Such is the story of the human race, the ongoing choice in favour of evil unless constrained by law or something higher. The defence of 'the devil made me do it' does not stand up. It is we who submit to the temptation, we who sometimes call upon the devil's help, consciously or unconsciously, as we pursue our self-interest and its negation of true love. Assist us he maybe will, but it is still we who make the fatal choice.

This negation is not about belief, but about action. It's about how we respond to the temptation to abandon love in favour of self-love. The devil in the form of a gaudy serpent is introduced as the Tempter in the Genesis story, not as the arch perpetrator. Adam and Eve are presented with three invitations to negation. They are the only possible three temptations in the universe, which does at least simplify matters. They are lust of the flesh, the lust of the eyes, and the pride of life. Gratify my bodily cravings, give me unlimited possessions and power, and make me a celebrity. Yet, the temptations appeared so innocuous. The tree was good for food, a delight to the eyes, and desirable to make one wise. And all the devil had to do was to question the goodness of God!

It is worth noting that Jesus faced these same temptations, not in a garden but in the wilderness that was the consequence of the Fall. In each case he came through and never once fell for the lie. Since this involved forty days of fasting for him (I think I once managed thirteen!) it was one of those life, death, resurrection cycles that had him return from the wilderness in the power of the Spirit, renewed, armed and able to beat the hell out of the devil. There's a lesson for us all here. Though you do not need to go on a long fast (no, really you don't!), you will have to learn to overcome temptation if you are to grow.

So, is that all the devil does, just tempts?

Well, it's been remarkably effective in ruining the human race so far. Yet, as we know from our own experience, the negation of love can take on a malevolence all of its own and that is why we are obliged to engage in a spiritual conflict. As the apostle Paul puts it:

For our struggle is not against flesh and blood, but against the rulers, against the authorities, against the powers of this dark world and against the spiritual forces of evil in the heavenly realms. (Ephesians 6:12)

Almost anyone who has had to oppose the aggressive intelligence of evil comes to realise at some point that they are dealing with more than simply a human adversary.

I am not suggesting for a moment that we take the sensationalist route of Hollywood horror movies, or that we succumb to paranoia, or become morbidly obsessed with evil. Let's not grant free advertising space to the opposition! Yet, there is what the Bible calls 'the mystery of iniquity'. Evil is irrational, malevolent and mad. The devil, if devil there be, is insane – a cosmic lunatic hell-bent on destruction because of his obsessive ego. Keep away from him if you want to stay sane! The writer Alexander Dostoevsky said, 'I do not know the answer to the problem of evil, but I do know love.' The choice seems clear.

Choose Freely

There is for God an unavoidable dilemma in this only possible universe. He must hate evil in all its forms, especially when it develops its own malevolence, but he must win us as those made in his image by our own free consent, otherwise that image could never be restored in us and we could never grow to be the greater people that he has in mind.

Human free will is not an illusion; we are not determined, and all attempts to say that we are prove to be unrealistic and usually simply absolve wrongdoers of personal responsibility. If it was once 'The devil made me do it', now it's 'My genes made me do it.' Any excuse for the ego!

However, we can be manipulated; we can be sold lies, we can be shaped by cultural forces, by educational propaganda, by subtle advertising. We can be threatened and cajoled; we can be overwhelmed by circumstances, but ultimately within ourselves we are still capable of making choices, and for most of us in normal life that is what we do. Yet even under the most abusive of regimes and in the face of monstrous evil, Alexander Solzhenitsyn could say,

'The simple act of an ordinary courageous man is not to take part, not to support lies! Let that come into the world and even reign over it, but not through me.'[11] Or, as Martin Luther King put it, 'The ultimate measure of a man is not where he stands in moments of comfort and convenience, but where he stands at moments of challenge and controversy.'[12] To resist evil, to overcome, even to reach out to God is our choice and ours alone, and he knows it and he honours it.

For this reason, although I am a man of peace who abhors violence and the stupidity of violence, I am not a pacifist. There are times when to love your enemy requires that you prevent him from doing actions that are self-destructive to his own soul and that are unloving towards others. The rapist and the psychopath must be stopped, as must the genocidal. But we must exercise the most careful heart-searching and know that our motives are pure. Violence easily begets violence; the victim becomes the victimiser of others.

This ideally is how our police forces should be motivated and our politicians and armed forces, too. That this is patently often not the case is a cause for regret, but that is the nature of a fallen world. That is why human freedom requires that the democratic debate must take place and those in power must be held accountable. It is why the right to peaceful protest, and acts of loving defiance, must be upheld – and why we should pray 'for kings and all those in authority, that we may live peaceful and quiet lives in all godliness and holiness' (1 Timothy 2:2). I am not a politician and even less a party follower, so I have little to say on this except, don't vote on the promises, vote on the person. Their known integrity, their serving of their constituents, their moral stature, is far more important to good government than mere party policies. Choose light to dispel darkness even in the moral murk of modern politics.

18. The Naked Self

Walk long enough on the water margin and you will find sooner or later that you begin to consider who it is that is doing the walking. Who am I really? It's easy to drown out this question by putting in the earpieces and filling your head with music. If you do, you might miss the moment and the opportunity to face this vital question. Even beginning to answer it requires us to remove distractions. Ignore it and we will struggle to go further in our quest for God and spiritual fulfilment.

Modernity, globalisation, political failure, untrustworthy authorities, existential loneliness, have all conspired to create an identity crisis in the West. Many of the former securities have disappeared. Young people struggle to find employment, and graduates complete their education saddled with huge debts. Trusting relationships are hard to come by. Marriages, if they happen at all, are often short-lived. Many choose simply to live together for as long as the feelings last. Who wants, who can risk, whole life commitment? Vast numbers of children grow up insecure for lack of knowing who they are in fluid family arrangements. They are over-stimulated and under-nourished emotionally. Increasing numbers of young people commit suicide. Antidepressant use has soared. People don't know who to trust any more. The institutions of government, church, police, school are viewed with suspicion. Politically, the world seems in constant crisis and extremists threaten us all. Newspapers and television feed this paranoia.

So, Who Am I Really?

It's hard to be honest with ourselves. We humans, unlike most animals, inhabit so many cloaks and masks that even to ourselves we appear as elusive figures on a misty stage. More shadow than self.

The secret of happiness lies in rediscovering our true selves in relation to the universe and to God. Yet stripping off the accumulated cloaks and masks is seldom comfortable. Adventurous spirits might begin the journey with enthusiasm, but many set out in trepidation, fearing the naked truth. It requires bravery, honesty and humility of heart and mind.

So, who am I and why does it matter? It's all very well to say, 'Be yourself.' But how may I be myself when I do not know the self to be? Why is me, me? What is this 'I am' that somehow came into being?

Genetically, it is fairly easy, but what if, as Teillard de Chardin said, we are not human beings having a spiritual experience; we are spiritual beings having a human experience?

Even so, whether materially or spiritually conceived, genes, *geist*, or both, it is reasonable to say that our birth self is essentially simple, insofar as it is pure, honest and true. The nurturing womb does not of itself either corrupt us or create a false persona. We are born innocent of experience, free of deceit, a true self. Naked we come into the world in more senses than just physical. Yet the moment of birth is precisely where the difficulty begins.

We entered a fallen world in which mask-donning is the norm. We soon learn to act according to the expectations of our parents, wider family and friends. The cost of social acceptance is conformity to their inherited cultural framework. Our freedom is within definite bounds with appropriate rewards and deprivations.

Sexual maturation adds another set of peer group pressures and state endorsed values, creating conflict between the often spiritual values of reticence and the secular values of licence. Passing from our teens to adulthood most of us have long since lost sight of our core self. We have an image to cultivate, a persona to project, a peer group to hang out with, a reputation to maintain. I am what I want my friends and family want me to be!

In Western society, consumerism promises spiritual and emotional fulfilment through acquisition. Advertisers seduce us with the notion that our identity depends on buying their product. How easily we delude ourselves into believing that doing so will give us self worth! We fail to see that without a discernible true self, our acquisitions are meaningless accretions. Our abundance of possessions becomes no more than another mask, cloaking us in unreality and superficiality, to compete with the other actors on the stage of life. In 'keeping up with the Joneses' we may well leave behind our selves.

Outstanding achievement, academic, sporting, financial, social, creative, even notoriety, much of it good in itself, may layer further masks and cloaks on those already existing. We grow ever more unreal even to ourselves, like the lonely clown, the insecure financier, the performance-driven athlete, the drug-dependent model, the image-driven celeb – all haunted by the fear of failure and rejection.

High achievers at least make money and perhaps consider the prize big enough to justify sacrificing their own selves to gain, if not the whole world, then at least a part of it. What of those who live vicariously through their heroes, where the ephemeral becomes more real to the fans than their own true selves. The delusion without the dough! Either way, the 'rich' and those who covet the life of the rich find it equally difficult to enter the world of reality – what some call the kingdom of heaven.

The search for being drives some to create mirage identities, online avatars. Not finding their true self they invent a false one to add to all the other personal falsehoods. We have something to hide. It's nothing new. Invented identity did not originate with the Internet; we began to hide from ourselves and from others in the Garden of Eden. And that in what should be the trusting context of marriage. That setting was also the origin of blame-shifting, or transference. We best maintain the guise by accusing others of hypocrisies that are also our own. In *The Crucible*, Arthur Miller called it 'daemonism' – blame others, lest they blame you.

Employing an analogy from carpentry, Jesus spoke of planks and specks in our eyes. Is this why we charge politicians, estate agents, journalists, bankers, advertisers, with hypocrisy, economy with the truth, when it is also true of us? As the occasion demands, we, too, don the heavy cloak of self-righteousness and the mask of innocence to avoid being found out.

Truth and truth about ourselves becomes ever harder to find under the welter of these false identities. Even religion will serve as a cloak. This applies not only to the reprehensible behaviour of paedophile priests, but to the whole business of external rituals, public performance, mantra and creed that allows us to feel better, when probably it should, at least for a season, have the opposite effect.

At root the way to see truly, to discover truth and life, is one that requires humility. It is only in the admission that we do not know that we first begin to learn. Admit that you know almost nothing about almost everything and you have started on the path to enlightenment.

A clue lies in Jesus' words, 'Truly I tell you, unless you change and become like little children, you will never enter the kingdom of heaven' (Matthew 18:3). Most certainly his words do not call us to abandon our reason and experience. Nor do they demand an unwholesome naivety on our part, or a surrender to a dominant tyrant. Rather, they require that we regain the honesty of the newborn child. Yet there is no simple going back; we must journey forward, stripping off the false ego until we are again as naked souls. This is the dying that alone can give us life. We must be truly 'born again', but it requires elective humility to be so honest, so pure of heart.

Let's remind ourselves that Jesus said,

Enter through the narrow gate. For wide is the gate and broad is the road that leads to destruction, and many enter through it. But small is the gate and narrow the road that leads to life, and only a few find it. (Matthew 7:13–14)

The gate is small and the way is narrow, not because it is narrow-minded, killjoy or puritan, but because it is honest. The false persona, the baggage of ego, will not pass through; we must travel light to find the light.

We will only find our true self in relation to God as we undergo the journey of mask-stripping, of returning to the spiritual nakedness of the newborn, so that we might be reclothed in truth. 'Know thy self and know thy God' is an age-old dictum that expresses the heart of what we were created to be. That is why it is important.

Sometimes this mask-stripping is forced on us by circumstances. Life may go terribly wrong for us. That could mean the loss of spouse through divorce, which might also include a loss of home and children. Many rough-sleepers are there because of broken relationships. It might be redundancy, the loss of career, or devastating illness that forces us to reappraise who we really are. This is an excruciatingly painful way that I would wish on nobody.

Then there is the chosen way. This is the mystical or contemplative route where we examine ourselves. Our journey so far may have already set us on the right path. This way is one where we begin mentally and emotionally to remove the masks and cloaks that constitute our persona – reputation, job, acquisitions, relationships, skills and talents, the lot, until we have stripped our ego of its power and delusions. Seeing that it is then largely a discardable mirage, we will begin to be in touch with our true selves. You may be pleasantly surprised at how happy and relaxed this makes you. This kind of inner work needs repeating many times throughout our lives.

Focusing on God in stillness until our thoughts settle is a good practice. The Hebrew word for God, Yahweh, was apparently a breathed word; a softened 'yah' on the intake, and a softened 'weh' on breathing out. The name of God is our first breath, and also our last. You might like to use this as a mantra for a period of time each day. I often do this as I go to sleep. Peter's first sermon on the day of Pentecost included the words, 'Everyone who calls on the name of the Lord will be saved.' 'Saved' is a broad and inclusive term, but in our context it might at least mean we will be saved from losing our most precious true self. As Jesus put it, 'What good is it for someone to gain the whole world, and yet lose or forfeit their very self?' (Luke 9:25).

I've also found great help in this journey by practising stream of consciousness daily writing. This is a preferably hand-written process where you pen about three sides of A4 a day with no planning or forethought, and no editing. It's not a journal; you just let your thoughts about life, and yourself, especially your self-perception, pour out as honestly as you know how. Nobody else will read this, except presumably God, and he may treat it as your first attempts at true prayer. Strange as it may seem, the only part of us that can really connect with God is our birth self, for this is the person he loved to create, and created to love.

19. Facing the Trials

God's great humanitarian project is to produce people who are adult enough to love him with the simple freedom of children – just as he loves us. Of course we may object and say we don't want his love. That is our prerogative – to go it alone, making what we can of ourselves until the final plummet that has no resurrection. But we must not fool ourselves into thinking that our autonomy is somehow our right or achievement. To make any proper sense of life, human beings must start at the point of death, because we all die, and many die at birth or shortly afterwards. So we really are lucky to be alive at all. Our lives, our very existence, are a grace gift from God whether we like it or not. If we have health and longevity as well then we should be doubly grateful. After all, why should any of us even exist? Do we really deserve any of our natural advantages? What will become of anything we have done? The company we worked for will have forgotten us within three months. We will grow invisible with age. Once the will is settled most of our relatives will get on with life without us.

Human Limitations

For all our progress, we humans have some well-known limitations. For a start, we all age and we all die. Thanks to advances in healthcare we have raised the age of death to the 'threescore and ten, and by reason of strength fourscore' for a lot more people, but for most of the human race it is still about right.

We are also limited in our powers. This gives us much pleasure as we watch Olympic athletes battle it out to knock 0.01 of a second off the 100 metres, but it also makes for an unequal world. This is hard for some educationalists to accept, but the simple fact is that some people will do far better than others, and although we should give all children equal opportunity, it will not produce equal results. One consequence of this is that the human race is largely divided between the haves and the have-nots.

What we can do is use our extraordinary powers of adaptation; we can control and manipulate the environment to our advantage like no other species. Our technological achievements are amazing and we are still only at the dawn of the technological age.

However, all this comes with a health warning. We are quite capable of annihilating ourselves. Weapons of mass destruction may not have existed in Saddam Hussein's Iraq, but we certainly have them, and so do many other nations, friendly or otherwise. Likewise, our untrammelled greed might lead to such environmental abuse that we destroy the ecosystem upon which our lives depend. It's sobering to remember that most of our food is grown in little more than a spade's depth of soil.

This brings us to our greatest weakness. Morally and spiritually we are largely inept, and that goes for just about every one of us. Indeed, those who most succeed at self-assertiveness and egocentricity, e.g. many celebs and politicians and business moguls, prove to be rather nasty people. They mostly turn out to be arrogant, jealous, callous, proud, dishonest, promiscuous, and licentious. Hardly the best models. All that they demonstrate is that wealth and fame and glory do not make us better people. Allow these values in the wrong political system and we have totalitarianism with all its manifest evils.

We fail by our own standards, let alone those that claim to be God's. We bleat about our rights more easily than we accept our responsibilities. We can't even get our religions sorted without some nutcase somewhere wanting to start a fight in the name of 'God' to force us into their way of behaving.

Am I being cynical? Trying to make us miserable? Not at all. This is life. 'Eat, drink and be merry for tomorrow we die.' Or maybe we might try, instead, to find out why we are here.

Death is the great leveller. It is also the most unnatural, natural act. We are meant to live for ever but paradoxically the only way to achieve that is by death. This is the point of helical theology. God lives for ever because he dies for ever and rises for ever. 'I am the Living One; I was dead, and now look, I am alive for ever and ever! And I hold the keys of death and Hades' (Revelation 1:18). He understands death, and because he has experienced human death for himself he is able to sympathise and help in the ways that humans need. This is why the songwriter, David, could write the most popular words quoted at funerals, 'Even though I walk through the valley of the shadow of death, I will fear no evil, for you are with me' (Psalm 23:4).

Dead Loss

We are a death-denying society and when it strikes we can scarce believe it, and especially if it appears to be a random act. There has to be a cause, someone to blame.

This is the basis for all conspiracy theories. People become convinced that a death was made to look like an accident, so they start accusing the most likely culprits. Anything but accept that accidents are in most cases accidents. Now I have no idea whether Prince Charles or someone high in government gave the nod to dispose of Princess Diana. I have equally no idea whether George Bush created 9/11 to justify a war on terror that would boost the American arms industry and justify imperial expansion. Both are theoretically possible and selective facts can be produced to make it look as though they are both true.

I am all for investigative journalism and I don't trust politicians or the aristocracy, or the rich and powerful. They all got where they are through extraordinary self-interest, but nothing will undo what has happened. Sometimes we may simply have to accept the reality of death, lest seeking for culprits becomes the denial of death.

If we can't easily accept the reality of life's end, we can neither accept easily those little losses, the smaller bereavements, along the way. I mean those personal losses that still leave people living but dead on the inside: the loss of a relationship, the loss of a job, the decline in health, or loss of a body part through accident or disease, the loss of friends through relocation, the failure to pass a driving test.

Trying to exonerate ourselves, blaming others, or going out and getting smashed, will solve nothing. Instead, we must learn to pass through the 'death' experience and be bereaved. Let the emotions come and pass through them. Until we do we cannot grow to be any better for the experience. We remain dead by not experiencing death. A transformed life is always the result of a transformed death.

Now this principle you will note is simply following the inbuilt cycle of God's world. It is then a healthy though painful path. But there is comfort and hope in it. Instead of drugging ourselves into emotional and spiritual zombie-dom we should seek the robust comfort of God, learn through the experience, and rise to a better inner life that will shape us for the future. The setback becomes the opportunity, but only if we undertake the journey.

The problem with a dualistic society is that we refuse the journey and, instead, project our fear onto others. These may be indigenous Indians in America, or refugees in Britain and Europe, or Jews, or Muslims, Mexicans, whoever. Only when we have hounded them to death, made the sacrifice, do we feel better. But it doesn't last, because the real problem is our immature selves, and our fear of death.

Those who talk about bereavement identify a random series of emotional states that include denial, anger, remorse, fear, sadness, confusion, loneliness, bitterness and despair. None of these are pleasant and it is tempting to avoid them or to fight them, but that only prolongs the bereavement. Let them happen and we will come through to a place of peace and reconciliation. At least, that's the theory.

In practice it's a roller-coaster ride with unpredictable ups and downs that will bring out the best and the worst in us, and the more naturally intense and passionate we are as people, the more we will feel it, as maybe our friends will, too. Incidentally, the ones who can't handle us in this state were never true friends in the first place.

One person will stick with us through it all, and that is Jesus. He has been there himself, and he understands and sympathises. When we hit rock bottom we will find he is the rock at the bottom. When we are high he is the view from the top. His Holy Spirit will be with us to strengthen and guide us so that we come through our trials. God gives people a future and a hope and although our lives may be different from what we expected, we will have grown closer to him. We will have a story to tell.

Some might sneer at this pious language of dependence. Faith in God is a crutch for the weak and spineless! It's for losers! Well, we are all losers in the end. Take your choice. Don't tell me those same people will refuse medical care, painkillers and other palliatives because they are too strong to need them. Do they not take aspirin and over-the-counter remedies when they have a cold – or at least a good slug of brandy? Do they never get by with a little help from their friends? Why should it be considered debasing if I say I get by with a fair bit of help from my friend Jesus? In the good times and in the bad.

Chronic Sickness and Trials

Enduring and watching others endure chronic pain and suffering, disability and deformity is one of the hardest challenges to face in life. Neither atheism nor other forms of linear theology seem to offer much comfort. Can helical theology do any better?

This is no academic matter for me. I have close family members and friends who have to bear lifelong sufferings. For them bereavement, loss, deprivation, is a daily reality. Like the apostle Paul in his sufferings their testimony is 'I die every day' (1 Corinthians 15:31). Yet these people keep going. If they die daily then somehow, by some grace, they rise daily. So is this just a futile daily cycle, this death and rising, or is there something more?

You might recall that early in this book I used the visual aid of a toy called the Slinky, a metal coil that illustrates the rising and falling, the undulations of life, when seen side on. Now, if you will, imagine this coil like an open spring rising upwards. Each turn of the coil is still a life, death and resurrection, but the process is all the time ascending.

Historically, Jesus was born, he died, and he rose again; but he also ascended. Now most illustrations of his ascent are rather stilted and have him statically taking an invisible heavenly elevator to the top floor. I am purely speculating at this point but since Elijah was carried away in a whirlwind (a helix, of course!), just maybe Jesus ascended in a rising spiral.

Whatever the manner of the ascension, the point is that the daily life, death, resurrection is not a futile cycle. It ascends. We grow, we rise, we come closer to God, and he to us.

Pious claptrap? Not when I see the amazing spiritual maturity in chronic sufferers who experience this process; a maturity, incidentally, of which they are almost entirely unaware. These people become role models of transformation; they become signposts to the real meaning of life. Often they are possessed of a deep inner joy and peace, a gentleness and grace that totally belie the reality of their sufferings. I see the face of Christ in them; for they, in a manner beyond my comprehension and through their pain, are in the presence of God. In spite of their bondage, they are free.

Paul writes,

Now the Lord is the Spirit, and where the Spirit of the Lord is, there is freedom. And we all, who with unveiled faces contemplate the Lord's glory, are being transformed into his image with ever-increasing glory, which comes from the Lord, who is the Spirit. (2 Corinthians 3:17–18)

This applies just as much to those who are prisoners of conscience as to those who are prisoners to their physical and mental ailments. Faith in Christ is tenacious in spite of circumstances. Multitudes of people are persecuted for conscience sake and Christians are the most persecuted people in the world with currently some 200 million Christians experiencing active persecution. Sadly, it's nothing new. The New Testament writer to Jewish Christians reported,

Many were tortured, refusing to submit, because their hopes were set on a better resurrection life. Others were publicly humiliated and flogged and chained up in gaol. Still others were stoned to death, beheaded and hacked to pieces. Many were reduced to destitution, wandering about in rags, poor, despised and abused because of their faith. The world did not deserve these good people, driven from society but still welcomed by God. (Hebrews 11:35–39 author's translation)

When Syrian Christians were being martyred in recent times their testimony was this: 'They think they are killing us, but actually they are planting God's seeds!' Nothing is wasted, even suffering, and all will be redeemed that can be. Death heralds resurrection.

Resurrection

20. Divine Infiltration

We are obliged to recognise that this is the only possible universe that a God of love could produce, and it is the one that we must live with, whether we like it or not, whether we understand it or not. Fun as it is to invent other worlds, and I have made my own modest contribution to that in my fantasy novels, our temporary escapism must bring us back down to earth. Those who can't do that generally need help from the people in white coats.

This universe contains not only the possibility of evil, but its actuality. Now whether we consider evil to be truly satanic or demonic, or political and moral, or simply the fact that things go wrong and accidents happen, is not the issue. More to the point is what can be done about it. What will God do about it? How does he respond to his own helical creation?

Once again, our bipolar, dualistic mindset lets us down. Either God should intervene and blast the bad guys, mend the broken, heal the sick, or he has abandoned us to a futile existence in a faulty creation, dropped us in the dirt and left us to find our own way out of it.

Neither is true. Love constrains God not to wipe out the planet; God loves the people made in his own image, and he will do his best to spare us. Love also will not abandon us to our own destruction. So, what is the alternative, keeping in mind that he will respect our free will and he wants us to grow up?

God's brilliant solution to the problem is divine infiltration.

God is remarkably subversive. Hints of his activity are everywhere but grace seldom smacks us in the face. Life is a treasure hunt for all, not a lottery for the favoured few to win because they have been given the lucky numbers. Even in the dramatic days of Moses with their earthquakes, volcanoes, burning bushes, Egyptian plagues, and the Red Sea crossing, God refuses to show his face unambiguously to his servant. It is still possible, albeit with great difficulty, to attempt an explanation of the events in naturalistic terms. Maybe. Tantalising!

Even when God visits the planet in person he does so subversively. Jesus is born to a young peasant girl in a backwater village far away from the centres of power. His arrival is witnessed by a few animals, some rough shepherds, and an overworked inn-keeping staff. Sometime later a few New Age astrologers turn up to give a bit of class to the proceedings, but that's about it.

What we know of Jesus' childhood and education is largely deduced from our knowledge of the cultural background of the times. He is not a childhood prodigy nor is he a teenage star. He begins his mission by disappearing into the desert and even when he returns in full charismatic power, he ignores the world leaders and focuses on the poor and needy, upon ordinary people like us. Always he refuses the invitation to lead an insurrection against the Roman overlords. As for his disciples, what a bunch of losers! Squabbling, disorganised, thick-headed, even they couldn't see clearly who their teacher was. The glory was veiled and only on the briefest of occasions was it visible to the naked eye. That is why Peter writes about the transfiguration of Jesus, 'We were eyewitnesses to his majesty.' Just a glimpse, but it was enough.

It has been well observed that the Christian faith is the only one that has an impoverished God, one who emptied himself of his glory. Rather than one who came down in shining splendour to impress us we have a God who came to join us in order to win us. In the film *Indiana Jones and the Last Crusade*, the Holy Grail is not the jewel-encrusted golden goblet but the simple wooden drinking vessel. Absolutely spot on.

Although I can understand as an artist the desire to produce expensive works of art to celebrate the glory of Christ, I am not at all sure he would be very impressed. Unlike the Egyptian pharaohs he did not order a glorious tomb nor did he insist on being buried with great wealth. Joseph of Arimathea, a secret and well-off follower, did his best but it proved to be no more than a very temporary, though well-meant provision. Jesus wasn't going to need that tomb for long!

There is another way in which God infiltrates our world – one that is neglected by our preference for dualism. We easily talk about God in heaven and Jesus coming to earth to show what God was like, but we as easily neglect the third dimension of the Trinity. We are more likely to talk about the presence of demons, or to believe in ghosts, than we are to be aware of the presence of the Holy Spirit. Yet the Holy Spirit is the ubiquity of God, he is the living presence of God in his world.

How might we recognise this presence? Well, seldom in fireworks. We are speaking of infiltration, not incandescence. He is the 'still, small voice' or 'gentle whisper' (1 Kings 19:12) after the storm. The Holy Spirit is in the sudden shiver of wonder; he is there in the unexpected warm glow, in the moment of enlightenment, in the surge of hope, in the inner peace in the midst of turmoil.

He is the One present in those epiphanies, those special moments where we experience a taste of God's splendour, like a transcendent moment of revelation that breaks in on our consciousness.

We call these epiphanies 'liminal' (like subliminal but without the sub), or threshold experiences because they provide an inkling, a glimpse, a taste of the heavenly parallel or non-visible universe. They might happen to anyone, anywhere, anytime and in any culture or political state. There are no barriers to the infiltration of the divine Spirit. They can happen to children and adults alike. They are profoundly emotional experiences but unlike mere emotional feelings that wear off once the event is finished, or we have sobered up, these are life-changing.

Liminal experiences are more common than we imagine and I could give you many examples including those from my personal life, but the problem in doing so is that they always sound so banal, mere descriptions of what is in essence indescribable and life-transforming. But you know when you have had one and it is evidence of God's nearness and his desire to reach you.

The Holy Spirit is described as the Strengthener or Fortifier in the Bible, the one who comes alongside to help. This world is far from totally bereft of God or goodness, and evil can and will be overcome. The infiltration of the Holy Spirit tells us that help is at hand, we can be strengthened on the inside, we can be comforted in our need and reassured for the future. That's why the apostle Paul could write to his deputy, 'For the Spirit God gave us does not make us timid, but gives us power, love and self-discipline' (2 Timothy 1:7).

Firework displays are impressive, especially over the sea, but they are not what we need when we are suffering. God has given us enough of that in the creation of the universe. Just open your eyes and look! So it's little use telling God that we will believe if he gives us a sign. How many more do we want? However, if we pray for the love, joy and peace of the Holy Spirit then that prayer is just about certain to be answered. Maybe we should give it a try.

This only possible and actual universe is one that of necessity is helical and follows a pattern of life, death and resurrection. That is the nature of God. Far from abandoning us to our fate he constantly infiltrates our world and if we learn how to look he is there for the finding.

21. The Way In

'Come on in, the water's lovely!' These words in my experience are usually uttered by those who learned to swim by breaking holes in the ice. Swimming off the British coast is certainly best done either in late summer or in a wet suit.

I learned to swim in a warm municipal swimming pool and warmth remains a precondition for me plunging into the briny. So let's imagine we have reached an unexpected shallow cove on which the sun has blazed for several weeks, and it is me, the warm-water-only swimmer, who is inviting you in. You might just risk getting your feet wet!

For me, this only possible universe presents us with an unavoidable choice: either we embrace the helical cycle or we refuse it. I'm sorry to put it that starkly but it does come down to just this. We may continue with our linear bipolar world view with its contradictions, conflicts and frustrations, or we take the life-changing step to harmonise with a greater reality. It's what we call a paradigm shift; you choose to live by different parameters, to do life differently. However, let me say at once that the seashore helps us here. We do not have to make the leap in one go if we aren't ready for that. It can be a transitional process – the third way of humbly feeling our way forward. You may wade in or plunge in. It doesn't much matter.

I invited you on a journey of exploration with a view to taking a fresh look at some neglected angles on life, to follow some fresh footprints, particularly concerning God and the problems associated with that. Now I must invite you on a journey within the journey – a journey that occurs inside us personally and one that only we can make for ourselves. I need to explain why, and what it involves because unlike reading this book it will require you to make a commitment. Yet without that step this will all remain theory. You may understand the concept but it will not change your life, will not resolve your dilemmas, will not bring you peace and hope.

Now, before you panic at the thought that I might be making an altar call or asking you to become a card-carrying member of a church, or 'give your life to Christ', I should explain that this is not primarily a religious invitation but a call to engage with the harmony of the universe and of the way that God works. It is to embrace for ourselves, however tentatively, this helical life, death, resurrection pattern of life. That this might take on a religious dimension, even a Christian one, will depend on what you want to do with your life. It is not for me to tell you. I hope that's fair enough.

Commitment

There are some matters in life that cannot be understood without commitment and experience. Nobody in their right mind would write a book on patience, for example. Patience is a virtue that can only be gained through experience. Likewise, the behaviourists who write pseudoscientific treatises on human love usually have no idea of what they are talking about simply because they are mere observers on the outside. All this nonsense about body language and mating rituals is laughable to anyone who is actually in love. It is something that can only be understood from the inside. That's why we turn to love songs and poems and sonnets rather than 'Ten Techniques for Pulling Birds' or whatever. Well, some youthful male clubbers whose minds rise no higher than their erections might, but no one with any sense!

Philosophers of science have long argued that it is almost

impossible for humans to study anything with total objectivity. For a start, we are all children of our time. The accidents of birth, race, gender, social standing, geography and our birth at a particular time in history are all outside of our control. We are placed where we are, and although we may make much or little of our lives we have virtually no say at all in the basic facts of our existence. How we set out and how we end is largely preconditioned and not much basic stuff changes for most people.

Even our way of doing science is largely determined by what business and what the military want, and what our culture desires for its pleasure and convenience. I'm not saying this is necessarily bad, it's just that we are not as free as we like to think we are. This will come hard to those who believe that they are fully in control of their lives and choices and can steer their ship of destiny at will. 'I am the master of my fate: I am the captain of my soul'[13] is actually laughable when you think about it.

I say this because commitment is already a reality for us; we are unavoidably committed to our existing culture, mindset and heritage, so it's no use saying that we fear commitment. That was established very largely the day we were born. What we fear is a change of commitment and the risks that this might entail. Yet without change none of us really grows and develops. Threshold, transitional, or liminal experiences are both unavoidable and essential. Birth itself is one such; so is going to school, entering puberty, getting your first adult job, falling in love, losing your virginity, getting married, having children. Likewise, along with these acquisitions come the losses, the bereavements. These, too, change our lives irrevocably. From then on we see things differently, and more fully.

C.S. Lewis used the homely analogy of the sun shining through a knothole in a dusty woodshed and illuminating the dust particles in the air. It's a perspective that is both pretty and capable of scientific analysis: otherwise invisible light reflecting off the dust particles to create a visible beam. Yet, says Lewis, there is another equally valid viewpoint and that is to stand in the beam of light yourself, to experience what it's like from the perspective of the dust particle, quite literally to see the light, to experience its dazzling glory first hand.

Such exposure to the light may dazzle you or give you a sun tan, or if you suffer from SAD, change your chemistry and lift your mood. Perhaps recalling his Damascus Road experience, the apostle Paul wrote, 'But we all, with unveiled face, beholding as in a mirror the glory of the Lord, are being transformed into the same image from glory to glory' (2 Corinthians 3:18 NKJV). In other words, seeing the light directly may change your life.

I had a similar and altogether milder experience myself when I was about sixteen years of age and was helping set up a campsite on a cliff top field near Dawlish in Devon. A light misty rain so familiar to English campers had begun to give way to sunlight in the distance. The result was the expected rainbow, but the difference was that this one ended on the field just a hundred metres from where we were erecting tents. Nobody else was prepared to do it, but I ran across the field and entered the rainbow.

It dispelled two myths. First, you can find the end of the rainbow. I did! Second, there is sadly no pot of gold. But, I saw a rainbow as I never had before, and wonderfully weird it was, too. The colours of my surroundings including my own skin took on surreal watery hues as I looked about me, and yet gazing up into the curve of the bow I saw that it had virtually no colour of its own from within.

This particular experience is of no great significance in itself, except to reinforce the point made by C.S. Lewis that it could only be had by making the commitment to enter. It opened up a different and perfectly valid way of seeing that was totally hidden to those who stood from afar. This was no madness on my part, no sacrifice of reason, and nor was it merely subjective – even less so, if millions of others shared a similar testimony of the rainbow's end, which for all I know they might.

So when secularists jump up and down with frustration because some of us claim experiences that they haven't had, it doesn't necessarily mean our experience is invalid; it's just that they lack the willingness to shift their butts and join us. The outside of the Royal Albert Hall is not particularly imposing, but enter inside and you will find an amazing arena complete with an impressive organ and a roof space seemingly filled with flying saucers, and you may hear some of the most awesome music on earth. The contrast between the outside and inside is dramatic, but you will have to enter the door to find out for yourself.

Jesus of Nazareth puts it another way when he said,

> Enter through the narrow gate. For wide is the gate and broad is the road that leads to destruction, and many enter through it. But small is the gate and narrow the road that leads to life, and only a few find it. (Matthew 7:13–14)

Now, here he is using 'reverse theology', something he did on numerous occasions. By saying that few will find it, he is not making a statement of fact so much as issuing an invitation to the curious. He is, if you like, provoking scientific exploration in a different direction to that of the cultural mainstream. Don't follow the crowd, particularly if it's obvious that the crowd is getting it wrong. In his context 'the few' were the faithful remnant of believing Jews, while 'the many' would prove to be those who had him killed.

Jesus described this as a narrow gate for several reasons. First, it filters out our excess baggage, a bit like an airport check-in desk. This is no bad thing because as with holiday trips, most of us take far more than we need, and on this journey you will need surprisingly little. Travel light.

His second reason was to tell us that however many there are in our party, we all have to pass through the security gate one by one. I've lost count of the number of people I have met who tell me, 'Oh, my brother's a vicar,' (I'm not, by the way), or 'My parents are churchgoers,' or 'I play badminton with a bunch of Christians. Nice people.' As if their association with religious people and their general goodwill towards them somehow meant they were on the right side. It doesn't, no more than me once being in a line-up to meet Princess Diana made me royalty. Noah's animals went in two by two, but with this gate it's one by one.

Jesus' third reason for his illustration is that the gate is easily missed, particularly by those who are tunnel-visioned, seeing only the bright lights of modernity. We are so used to hurtling down the motorway of life and looking for main junctions that we can miss this all-important side turning and even should we spot it we will have all sorts of doubts and questions about whether it is the right road. Worse still, everyone else will carry on down the motorway, while your satnav instructs you to 'turn around as soon as possible'! One of the problems of techno-modernity or digi-modernity (which incidentally has long since replaced post-modernity) is that for all its diversity it is remarkably uniform in content, values and usage. It produces social, moral and spiritual conformity. If you are to find a new way then you will have to break away from the status quo.

Imagine if you will an unimposing garden gate half hidden by the undergrowth and barely signposted. You need to have your eyes open, you need to be curious. Desperation may help too, but most of all you need to become like a little child who is small enough to spot it. It's what Jesus meant when he said, 'Truly I tell you, unless you change and become like little children, you will never enter the kingdom of heaven' (Matthew 18:3). It's children who find the hole in the fence, the little gate in the undergrowth. Adults are apt to walk right by holding to their view of reality as though that were the only truth and in the process failing to discover the path of life. So, how will we recognise this gate when we find it? What clues does it provide to say this is the right one?

Death Gate, Life Gate

The most obvious clue is that it probably doesn't look like the right one. It doesn't appear particularly religious. The gate to life isn't glitzy; it doesn't advertise itself with sale offers or 'two for the price of one, buy one get one free' enticements. It doesn't promise to remove your wrinkles or make you irresistible to the sex of your choice. It may seem to be inviting you to your own funeral rather than to a party.

This is exactly what we should expect because if we are to embrace the helical way of life then our former life must die in order to enter a new life. The old judgements, the former rules of existence, have to be abandoned in the act of humility that creates the zone of grace and enables us to receive the mercy of a fresh start. In the Christian version this path is often enacted in adult baptism where the death is represented in being immersed in the water. Yet it is more than a one-off spiritual ritual. Entering this re-creative helix is meant to become a pattern of life, whether you have undergone a physical baptism or not. In fact, unless it produces a new lifestyle, baptism is as good as worthless.

Let me give you a simple example at this point.

I did not learn to swim until I was about ten years of age and I well remember going to the swimming baths and trying to swim ten metres. I learnt the strokes and pushed off from the side as hard as I could, but every time I did so my foot would touch the bottom after two-and-a-half metres or so. Then I discovered the secret. Until now I had tried to master the water and in so doing I had blocked its own intrinsic power. The moment I surrendered to the water by taking a deep breath and bending my stiff neck so that my face was under the surface, I released the magic of buoyancy. I swam ten metres with no problem. When I attempted twenty-five metres I needed to take more than one breath. This required me to raise my head above the water but then to recommit myself to the 'drowning' that once more released the buoyancy.

Nowadays, of course, I don't even think about it when I go swimming. Abandonment to the buoyancy of water, the surrender of land dwelling to water dwelling, is now automatic. My 'death' releases the life of a swimmer every time, as it does for anyone who can swim. It may be worth noting that babies and little children find this easiest of all, a point that Jesus of Nazareth would probably endorse!

Now I wish to sympathise with you if all this feels uncertain, threatening even. Passing through this gate, making a commitment, choosing the path of humility, is for most of us to enter the twilight zone. We are walking an unfamiliar shore in the dusk; we are on the boundary where nothing is quite familiar and nothing seems certain. Doubts and fears will assail us as we contemplate the path ahead that looks so unpromising and faltering. Can this really be the solution to my problems? Will this approach resolve my dilemmas and my questions about God and suffering, and everything else? Whatever logic the case has had until this point is now swamped by uncertainty.

I learned in my mountain-walking days that you often have to go to the edge to find the right path. I equally know that the edge is the most creative, life-generating place to be; change and movement never happen at the centre but always on the fringes. Ironically, the narrow gate broadens your mind! To go tripolar is an exponential leap into a zone of infinite possibilities; it is to walk the unlimited way of love and constant renewal and personal growth. The gate is narrow only in the sense that it abandons all the false and inadequate options in favour of one that is far better. What looks like a way of death turns out to be the path of life.

That said, you will be taking a step of faith; so we had best take a look at what we mean by faith, and by doubt.

22. The Faith Experiment

We hear quite a lot about faith and faith communities these days. People talk about the need to believe, and though they may argue about what to believe, faith remains at the heart of, well, faith. But just what is it? In particular, is faith blind, i.e. wholly without evidence? Do we embrace faith as something that by definition we have no hope of proving? Do we lose our marbles because there is nothing to think? Is faith no more than naive optimism, wishful thinking, a leap in the dark in the hope that someone will catch us?

Many people believe that faith and reason are simply incompatible opposites, but this is just the usual bipolar, dualistic, way of thinking. Why should they not go hand in hand? That is precisely what we find in the greatest expression of God's humility, in Jesus of Nazareth. In him the spiritual (the zone of faith) and the physical (the zone of reason) are perfectly joined, and the result is a wondrous work of art. The eyewitness apostle John makes this observation.

> The eternal Word became an actual human being and lived here among us. We saw his true splendour, the splendour of the only Son of the Father. Through him all the mercy and all the truth of God have become available to us. (John 1:14 author's translation)

It seems to me that faith is based on reasonable assumptions, just like everything else in life. For example, I reasonably assume that Australia exists even though I have never been there. Sure, it could all be an elaborate hoax, but it is unlikely. Nearer to home, I reasonably assume that my chair will support my weight, that my wife and children love me, that my friends are still my friends, that antibiotics kill germs and the water is safe to drink. None of these things deny rationality but trusting in any of these circumstances is still an act of faith, because I cannot know absolutely the consequences of any particular action. In other words, life cannot be lived without an element of risk.

I have met people who seem obsessed with eliminating risk from their lives. They live in mental boxes of their own creation, by definition narrow-minded, insecure, unable to love freely and desperately insecure. To those of us living in the risk-ridden real world their lives appear tragic.

So can I tell you that making the paradigm shift to embrace the life, death, resurrection cycle – particularly the 'death' part – is wholly without risk, perfectly safe, and guaranteed to work for you? Of course not! I offer no guarantees that this will work in your particular case, this is not advice or counsel, terms and conditions may apply, this is not offered as any form of treatment, and any decision you make is entirely your responsibility and at your own risk. So much for legal disclaimers!

Risk, uncertainty, is a natural part of life, and it is no different here. Indeed, I would be insulting your intelligence if I did not invite you to take the risk. One of the problems with some types of conversion theology is that they require a once and for all decision on our part, whereas I see it more as a faith experiment that may be repeated and examined until we are sure. That was certainly my own experience. I began an exploratory journey along an undulating and winding path, discovering what it was like to live according to a helical pattern. Rather than being told that my destiny was fixed, I was invited to follow a trail.

Others, including myself, can trace a pattern to their lives in retrospect. There is an evident plan and path; we have an evidence-based story to tell that indicates to us a divine hand on our lives. But it didn't seem like that at the beginning. Following the trail was an act of faith, like any scientific quest, or exploration of a new land. My choice was to explore, to find the narrow gate, i.e. the one solution to the puzzle that made all the equations work, and that had the artistic elegance of being right.

Why did I bother? That's a longer story, but it boils down to the fact that I could see that the street beliefs didn't work. I sensed and desired that there would be more than this. Like Julie Walters in the film *Educating Rita*, I wanted to sing some better songs. And, yes, I have found the way and I can now see that every circumstance led me to this, so long as I kept being honest and curious. That's how God's sovereign grace works.

Looking back, I can trace a decidedly guided path that I visualise as a winding silver thread, even a divine destiny at work, but the decision to continue, to interact with God, to make choices, has been truly my own. My faith experiment has been based on the reasonable evidence of observing the correlation between nature, the Bible and my inner psyche and finding these formed a trustworthy pattern for living. Likewise, I have been privileged to witness some largely unknown but amazing examples of how faith works.

This has made it fairly easy for me to dismiss the charlatans who are in the religious business for personal gain, and likewise the secular charlatans who write novels and treatises purporting to claim that the whole thing was made up by the church. They are simply wrong and intellectually dishonest.

My journey led me to Jesus of Nazareth. In spite of my aversion to religion, I found in him the perfect model of what the helix is all about, and I came to realise that he was authentic in describing himself as the Way, the Truth and the Life. He became for me the knowability of God, and very good at it he is, too!

I am not a very good example. Like most people, I have my ups and downs, my failures, my inconsistencies. I am most definitely a work in progress and not the finished article, at best a not very good follower of Jesus. So I will not boast of what I have experienced as though I have reached some esoteric higher consciousness by my own doing. For me it is all a gracious gift from God that I could not possibly earn. The gift is offered freely to us all and unconditionally. The journey is about daily and continually drawing on it.

My reasonable and enquiring faith has allowed me to extrapolate consistently beyond what I can observe and test. I can now see with the eye of faith – sanctified imagination based on divine revelation – what is otherwise invisible; I can live with a fuller reality, and experience the relational presence and empowerment of God in my life. The old Deism of a distant, disinterested God, the aridity of secularism just seems so empty, thin and desiccated, like the surface of a barren moon. In spite of at times enormous difficulties and challenges, I live in a promised land that flows with milk and honey, a fulfilment of Jesus' words: 'I came so that everyone would have life, and have it in its fullest' (John 10:10).

Jesus the Way has proven for me the right track to follow. I have found the way out of Plato's cave of shadows and illusions not through philosophy but through faith. I have found the pearl of greatest price, the true treasure, the philosopher's stone, the Holy Grail, and all this for tentatively entering the narrow gate!

All I can say of my faith journey, my 'conversion', is that I crossed a number of bridges over the course of time and let them rot. Experience is cumulative. Theologians will tell you that you've got the lot the day you say the formula, as well they may, but my theology remains that of the street: you've got to walk it and find out for yourself.

On our beach you may find quite a lot of flotsam and jetsam, and treasure seekers with their metal detectors and earphones. Most of what they uncover turns out to be beer caps, rusty nails, tinfoil and the like, but every once in a while they hit gold. Our search requires elementary sorting or discernment, but there is gold awaiting the persistent seeker. For me, Jesus' way and my relationship with him, however tentative, is the gold. I hope it might be the same for you, but as always it's your call.

Doubts And Fears

Every so often I come across super self-assured people who seem to have an innate ability to make me feel inadequate. They never have problems, they only have solutions. Every setback is an opportunity. Their clothes are smart and their cars are as buffed to perfection as are their bodies, and they can reel off a long list of their achievements and acquisitions. Faith for them is unassailable self-confidence and they could sell you your mother's eyes.

I am not like that. My background is that of an urban peasant with all the insecurities of poverty and working-class disempowerment. To make matters worse, I have an artist's melancholic temperament mixed together with an impossible drive to achieve perfection with mediocre talents. So my work is never good enough and half the time I finish up giving it away or hiding it. Some people are natural clothes hangers; with me clothes just hang. I have no institutions to my name, no international movements or grand buildings; just a few wonderful people whose journeys I have for a while been privileged to share in. Doubts and fears come with the territory.

I share this because some people wonder if they can keep up a faith-based life and so fear to take even a first step. They hold back because of doubt and finish up doing nothing. The classic Christian response is to say that it doesn't depend on you holding on, but on God's unbreakable grip. But I'm not so sure it's that simple, not least because the Bible contains a fair number of warnings that seem to say, 'You had better hold on, or you'll drop right in the cesspit!'

So what is the truth?

The truth is simply that God never abandons us, even though sometimes it seems that way – and that includes the times when we doubt everything, when we fear the future, when we've blown the present. Remember those undulations. Life goes up and down.

It is helical: life, death, resurrection. Doubt times, fear times, messed-it-up times, are the downturn, the death that eventually will emerge as resurrection life. Like champagne corks at sea, you can push us under but we will resurface. That is the nature of this tripolar life, that is why I have no hesitation in saying, give it a go. Ultimately, you have nothing to lose and everything to gain.

People of faith are real people; very few of them live trouble-free lives with consistent faith and perfect behaviour. I certainly don't! We have embarked on a journey and we have yet to reach our destination, that's all. Life can be very testing. Nobody starts out on this journey because they're good enough or want to fulfil their personal ambitions. The perfectly self-contained and successful who have already solved all their problems need not apply; indeed, they will see no point in applying. Jesus welcomed everyone, but in the sure knowledge that some considered themselves too good for him. 'The fit and healthy don't need a doctor, but the unwell. I didn't come to invite perfect people to turn to God. I came to invite sinners' (Luke 5:31–32 author's translation). Doubts and fears are as good a reason as any for paying a visit to the divine Doctor.

Action

Faith is an action word; it is not simply a state of mind, like optimism. You can't learn to swim from a book. Nor is it a system of beliefs, or a moral code. Faith means doing something, committing yourself to a course of action. In our context, it means at the least simply incorporating the death, the humility element, into our thinking. It may mean a wholehearted decision to become a follower of Jesus and seek a relationship with God. Perhaps you are somewhere in between. Wherever you are in your journey I recommend that you act on what you do know, not on what you don't know. At all costs retain your personal integrity.

I remember a young woman getting baptised on impulse at an emotionally charged meeting. Within a week she had renounced the whole business, and I could understand why. She had acted way ahead of where she was, had taken an existential leap, rather than a step of faith. To my mind she should have been refused baptism until she knew more about what it involved, which is why many churches offer enquirers' courses, the best known of which is Alpha, but there are several others.

One of the things I like about Jesus' teaching is that he did his best to stop people following him unless they had counted the cost. That's no bad thing, particularly for those of us without a religious background who will not understand half of what is going on, anyway. So step through the gate at the level you are currently able and see where the road takes you.

23. Restoring the Conversation

We set out to challenge the default street theology that we call Deism, the belief that God has no interest in us, that the universe is a closed circle allowing for no divine intervention. In its place, we have suggested that God is alive and well and intimately involved with his creation, that his 'shape' is that of an open helix, one that eternally pulsates to the vibrant rhythm of life, death and resurrection. This rhythm follows the notes of justice, mercy and humility, which is the heart of true love, and invites us into a world that resounds with amazing grace when we enter it. Now I freely admit that this is a 'best fit' and it doesn't answer everything, but nonetheless for me at least it answers most of my questions and gives coherence to the rest. I hope it does the same for many of my readers. To take this route is a step of reasonable faith and humility, a narrow gate that leads to the path of life and truth.

For most of us the way to enter that gate is simply to start praying. That shouldn't surprise us: a God who is near is surely one with whom we can communicate and who wishes us to do just that. You don't create people in your own image only to have nothing to do with them! Deism is logically false. Nor do you treat them as your playthings, the toys of the capricious Greek gods on Mount Olympus. You want, like a good parent, to listen to your children, even if in their early developmental years they talk a load of drivel.

Daring to Pray

It doesn't do to admit that we pray. It suggests weakness or even insanity, especially if we claim to hear back! Surely people who make such claims are deluded, stark staring bonkers. We should probably lock them away. This has always been a favourite ploy of totalitarian regimes for dealing with dissidents, and you can always find a perverse, terrified or ill-educated psychiatrist who will sign a medical form to give some hypocritical credence to this legal farce.

Intelligent atheists will want to distance themselves from this rubbish and recognise that, even if they choose not to themselves, to be human is to pray and sometimes to identify an inner voice that guides and helps us through life. Most people have some experience of this. Only when the voice is telling them that they can fly without wings from a high-rise block of flats or that they should slaughter all the grannies in their road should we be worried. The line between eccentricity, genius, religious devotion and madness may be thin but it is absolutely recognisable by all sane people.

For all that, there remains a certain embarrassment about admitting we pray and even worse to admit we attend a prayer gathering. We prefer to use longer words like meditation or contemplation; we seek out 'third places' or even 'sacred space'; we engage with the mystery of the cosmos, or the Gaia, or the life force; we practise yoga. Now I've a lot of sympathy with this. After all, people are taking steps towards a spiritual life, and that deserves commendation. However, the danger is that it may require no humility on our part, no expression of abandonment or need, no dependence. We remain in control. In other words, our actions may stay firmly in the zombie zone of the spiritually undead and, therefore, the un-resurrected. We must remember Jesus' words about the necessity of seeds dying before they can bear fruit – and prayer is a form of dying.

Even when we do admit to praying, daring to use that socially naff word, we may still get it wrong.

Popular New Age self-help books see prayer simply as a

mechanism for self-realisation; connect to the god/goddess within, or utilise the underused right-hand side of your brain to discover solutions that your left brain can't see. If not that, then pray as a means of articulating your fears and worries, a technique for externalising your anxieties so that they don't become neuroses.

Then there is the religious approach suited to those who are much more left brained and need a logical structure to their lives. The words, the postures, the rituals, assume great importance. Indeed, their acceptance by the divine being often depends on getting these things right. Prayer becomes a matter of self-control, of skill or technique, of carefully articulated phrases and correct gestures.

Also among the 'technique' of prayer types are those who believe we may order God about, demanding and commanding, often in a loud voice that he does what he has apparently promised to do. There are two versions of this: those who do it in the name of religious faith (I am most familiar with those of Christian persuasion), and those who are into 'cosmic commanding', telling the universe to obey our wishes. Duh! Power freaks, every one of them!

Whatever traces of reality there might be in the above, they are all selfish approaches and they don't wash with the living God. Prayer is about communication between us and him. It is essentially relational. That is why the perfect prayer that Jesus taught begins 'Our Father'. Even on earth we seldom get our way when we demand that our parents do as we tell them, and it is just plain stupid to compose special forms of words with which to address them. So why would this work with God?

Here we are at a beachside refreshment hut. We approach the proprietor.

'Wouldest thou of thine eternal beneficence grant unto thy humble supplicant the water of life infused with the oriental herb of refreshment, yea, even *Camellia Sinensis*?'

'D'you what, mate?' he replies. 'Foreign are you? Oh, I get it. You mean you would like a cup of tea!'

Plain English works best with God, too.

As for, 'I'm speaking to you, Mum, so that I can discover the inner me, and I demand a new car' – forget it!

Now let's deal with the criticism brought by those who don't understand this. Most commonly they want to charge us people who pray with arrogance: 'If God really has made a universe of the size we think it is, then how can he possibly be interested in a speck of dust like you?' This, you will recognise, is the un-renewed mindset of a Deist – God is just too big and too distant to bother.

Answering it is a piece of cake. It is precisely because God is capable of creating and managing a universe this large that he has no problem listening to us and billions of others like us who wish to talk with him. A little deity might have difficulty keeping up, but not the God who is poetically described as saying,

'Heaven is my throne, and the earth is my footstool. What kind of house will you build for me? Where will my dwelling-place be? Have I not made everything and brought it all into existence?' declares the Lord. 'These are the ones I look on with favour: those who are humble and reflective in spirit, and who are thrilled by my words.' (Isaiah 66:1–2 author's translation)

God in his divine humility is prepared to listen to my prayers, if I will have the humility to open my mouth.

The first time I prayed it was weird. I did it out loud and could only hear the sound of my own voice. I would not have wanted anyone else around me. It was an awkward experiment, an act of humility that I might never do again and never admit to ever having tried. There was no answer; no angelic lights, no voice in my head, no skywriting, no divine pat on the back. That's not how it works, as I quickly learned. To be honest, it felt a bit like going to a doctor and being told to explain why you were there, just as all your symptoms disappeared!

Why did I carry on? Partly because I had more than an inkling that I was on the right track, and because in science the first experiment seldom yields the desired result, and in art the first sketch is not the masterpiece. You keep on until you find the secret. In the Garden of Eden, God used to meet with Adam and Eve to engage in conversation with them. Communication was easy, the way a parent might speak with young children, for that precisely was their innocent state even though their bodies were presumably adult and sexually mature. The Fall broke that ease of relationship; from then on prayer on our part, and hearing God speak back, has been fraught and frankly hard work like everything else worth doing in life. We have, like the prodigal son, wandered into the far country and wasted our lives. Only when we come to our senses – and sometimes that may be forced on us by dire circumstances – do we attempt to pray.

This difficulty is what has produced our confused approach to prayer. Maybe it is necessary. Perhaps it is only by going through the learning process – remember the helical pattern – that we can ever become adult enough to speak to God properly. Restoring the lost conversation is at first an effort and there is much to learn, but it will become easier, more familiar and natural until you hardly realise that you are praying at all. Even silence becomes communion, the way long-time lovers can drive for miles without speaking but still be in absolute heart-to-heart communication.

Anger at God

I can't remember the subject of my first attempt at prayer, except that I was enquiring rather than enraged. That was to come later. However, you may feel so angry that you really struggle to utter even a single prayer. This anger arises most commonly because we are frustrated by our own impotence and finding no one else to blame we take it out on the one who is supposed to be able to do everything. Like many blokes I am good in a crisis provided I can do something to help or to fix the problem. It's when I can't that I get uptight and start lashing out. Or maybe we feel angry because we think God is punishing us or our loved ones without any good cause, or that he has deliberately dropped us in the cesspit just for the hell of it.

I suspect from the tone of their writings that some militant atheists are emotional atheists. At some point they have ceased to believe because of some traumatic event that they have not handled well. Rather than admit this, they rationalise their case and construct elaborate non-sequitur arguments in favour of denying God's existence. Well, I could create those same arguments but I've stopped doing so because I think there are better ways of dealing with our anger at God than simply responding in pique.

My suggestion is that we recognise the anger for what it is; personal frustration. If it helps, have a good old rant at God. I remember once walking for a couple of hours in the pouring rain shouting and complaining to him about everything that frustrated me. I expect my language was pretty ripe at the time, too. Was I struck by a thunderbolt? Punished for my insolence? Overwhelmed with a terrible Presence? Struck dumb? No, of course not. The Creator and Sustainer of the universe is more than able to cope with my infantile tantrums! He just waits until we've got it out of our system and are free to have a proper conversation. That for me usually begins with the word 'Sorry'.

Why? Because God demands that? No, because that's how I normally respond to people who love me and whom I have upset or spoken out of turn to.

Anyway, arguing with God is a bit daft when you think about it. As C.S. Lewis put it, 'Perhaps we feel inclined to disagree with him. But there's a difficulty about disagreeing with God. He is the source from which all your reasoning power comes: you couldn't be right and he wrong any more than a stream can rise higher than its own source. When you are arguing against him you're arguing against the very power that makes you able to argue at all: it's like cutting off the branch you're sitting on.'[14] So true!

How to Pray

Part of the genius of the Lord's prayer, the one that Jesus taught his followers in response to their question about how to pray, lies in its universality. Anyone can pray it whatever their ethnic, religious or cultural background. If you can call God your Creator, then you can pray, 'Our Father'. As the last prophet of the Old Testament says, 'Do we not all have one Father? Did not one God create us?' (Malachi 2:10). This prayer of Jesus is set in the context of a talk that is usually called the Sermon on the Mount, which he opens by stating quite simply that everyone is welcome in his company just as they are. By this he meant that we have no need to improve ourselves before we are fit to speak with him.

That is certainly true when it comes to the mechanics of prayer. There is no set way. You may stand, sit, kneel, drive, walk. I find walking is a good way for me, so walking the seashore is good for a human/divine conversation. But it's not for everyone. Find your own 'sacred space' if you are just starting out, but you'll find after a while that all space is sacred and you can pray anywhere.

Now if Jesus taught us how to pray I would assume that the Lord's prayer is highly likely to be answered if we pray it. Just to remind you how it goes, in case your school failed to teach you, it reads:

Our Father in heaven,
hallowed be your name,
your kingdom come,
your will be done,
on earth as in heaven.
Give us today our daily bread.
Forgive us our sins
as we forgive those who sin against us.
Lead us not into temptation
but deliver us from evil.
For the kingdom, the power,

and the glory are yours
now and for ever.
Amen.

You could do worse than pray this just as it is written, as countless millions do every day across the globe. Or better, you could come with what you want to say or ask and see where your request fits, or maybe doesn't fit, into a line of this prayer. For instance, if you are sick, your prayer may fit in with 'Your will be done' or it might fit with 'Lead us not into temptation' or 'Deliver us from evil'. You choose.

Approaching it this way prevents the prayer from becoming a superstitious religious mantra and, instead, lets it remain part of a thoughtful conversation. We are beginning to discuss our situation with God instead of treating him as an app on our smartphone. Remember the goal is to restore the loving relationship that was lost in the Garden of Eden.

This growing intimacy is why we pray; that is why it is unhelpful to approach God with our shopping list and why we get so few answers to such lists. It's as though we have fallen in love and on the second date we come with a list of requirements: I want you to wear blue, give me £1000, and a new car, fix my bad knee, heal all my diseases, kill all my enemies, find me a parking space every time, make my friends like me and give me this week's lottery numbers. Even if the object of your love could do these things, they wouldn't. In fact they would be quite justified in walking out on you there and then!

Love is cultivated without demands. It is equally true the other way as well. God doesn't say to us, 'OK, now you've started praying you must do the following: stop looking at pretty girls (or boys); give up smoking, drinking, football, the *Sun* newspaper, masturbation, nice clothes and smart cars.' That is the way religion works; it is not the way a relationship develops. I can hardly stress this enough. Jesus welcomes us as we are and begins the process of relationship building, just as we must, also. Lifestyle changes occur as a consequence of the relationship; they are not the means of securing the relationship.

The changes that most matter occur almost unconsciously and they are like the blending of musical instruments into harmony as two musicians play together. The process of harmonisation is gradual and, depending on who we are and our starting point and our circumstances, our rate of change will vary. We may or may not become perfect in this life, but that doesn't mean the process is wasted. An unfinished picture is better than no picture at all.

Does Christ change as well? In the sense of perfection, no, but in the sense of getting to know us, of his being intimately involved in our life journey then, yes. His experience of me and of all other believers adds to his knowledge base, and he is enriched by that reality. This is grace; this is the humility of God. Does he who owns everything need me? No. Does he want me? Most certainly, yes. And you, too.

Now this experiential reality is not what most of us are told lies at the heart of the Christian faith. We are taught that it is a belief system like any other religion, or a holier-than-thou morality. But it isn't, except at the most superficial level. It is about discovering a renewed conversation with God that energises and enlightens us and, through the simple act of humility, releases a renewed and transformed life. Nor is this for the rare super-saint, but it is the actual experience of countless numbers of ordinary people across the world every day.

24. Hearing God's Voice

Prayer, real prayer, is a two-way communication. That's why some of the best praying is simply listening, contemplating or meditating. The purpose of which is to hear God speak to us. But how does God speak? Do you hear voices in your head? Does he leave messages? How would you recognise his voice, anyway?

The best answer I can give is that it will be appropriate to who you are. We are all wired differently and if God is to be personally involved in our lives then we should expect him to take that into account. A quick reading of the Bible stories will illustrate this.

Abraham is about to follow the cultural norm of sacrificing his firstborn son when he audibly hears an angelic voice that delivers him from such pagan barbarism. Jacob hears God in a vivid dream. Moses hears God through the phenomenon of a burning bush. We read stories of volcanoes, earthquakes, and quiet breezes that all somehow convey the voice of God to people.

Prophets – the creatives – speak the voice of God through music and song, poetry and prose, drama and art, proclamation and miracle. They have visions, dreams, interpretations of dreams, transcendent shifts in consciousness without the use of drugs or special techniques. Sometimes the voice of God is so obvious that it needs no special 'word'; at other times it is counter intuitive. God speaks through nature, through circumstances, through the Bible, through silence and sound, through angels and preachers, as an inner voice, an intuition, through particular emotions – even through pain.

God is always speaking; all we have to do is keep our eyes and ears and hearts open. We may call it 'cultivating the Presence'. Prayer does this better than anything else I know. We can confidently offer our prayers and even if we hear nothing at the time, we can expect that God will speak through any of the above means as we go about our daily business. The point is, he does not speak in isolation from other things that are going on in our lives; the 'seed' usually falls into prepared ground.

I must stress that looking to God is not the same as looking to the stars. Astrology works by autosuggestion, by planting generalisations to trigger apparent confirmations, having already preconditioned people to believe that their personality type is determined by their star sign. Frankly, in my opinion, it's rubbish! You'll be better off listening to the Creator of the stars rather than some ancient Babylonian-Egyptian superstition. A superstition that is based on a few arbitrary and imaginary two-dimensional sky drawings of stars that are in reality light years apart and can have no possible impact on life on earth. Sorry if that messes up your horoscope!

So how do you know it is the voice of God and not just your own imagination? 'God' apparently tells some lunatics to commit genocide! Any number of people locked up in institutions or under care in the community regimes claim to hear 'God' telling them to do insane things. People are persuaded by rhetoric to give away all their money, or invest their savings in a corrupt business venture, or get the lottery numbers by throwing dice, and claiming that 'God' told them to do it!

It's simpler than it seems, though experience will enable you to become more discerning. Remember that God is love, so he will not tell you to do anything that is unloving, that does harm to yourself or others, for 'you are to love your neighbour as yourself'. He will not feed your vanity or greed or lust, nor will he tell you to break the Ten Commandments. He will not guide you to exact vengeance, kill heretics, or start religious wars or mount hate campaigns.

He will, however, lead you in the paths of right living; he will provide you with wisdom if you care to ask; he will bring you inner peace and assurance. There will be times when you will receive guidance that resolves a dilemma. Sometimes you will receive remarkable faith for a miracle. On occasions his answer will come in the shape of a person who can help you, or a change of circumstances over which you had no control. It's all a matter of ask, relax, and listen. In the Old Testament, people sometimes threw dice or drew lots to determine the will of God. All that is superseded in the New Testament. Now people listen to the inner voice of the Holy Spirit and compare notes with others whom they can trust. So much more relational, but that's what it's all about.

Silent Times

I have known people who have experienced a remarkable sense of relief once they have started this conversation with God. For some it becomes a powerfully emotional experience complete with tears and euphoria; others just feel calmer and better ordered. There are those, too, who avidly want to know everything they can about this new way of doing life. They read the Bible, and books about the Bible; they devour devotional books with all the zeal of new converts, and they will testify that their lives have been transformed. God is near, he is their Friend and Companion. Life is wonderful!

I am no cynic; I have had and do have all these experiences in my own life, and I can celebrate the new-found joy of others with the best of them. However, I do know that at some point and at various seasons throughout life, the euphoria will die down, prayer will become difficult and dry, God will apparently not answer prayers, and worst of all he will seem distant. At such times, you might well ask whether the Deists were right after all.

All of a sudden, any confidence you may have had in God's love seems to evaporate. Perhaps God doesn't want you, anyway. You have made a fool of yourself, you are not good enough, your friends were right, you were not cut out for all this. Back to the 'eat, drink and be merry, for tomorrow we die', world. Let's get smashed, get laid, get the old life back. All that self-improvement requires far too much effort to sustain. Old habits die hard; why fight them any longer?

The first thing to say is that this is not uncommon; in fact, it's probably normal. Some have described these experiences as the dark night of the soul, or 'dog days'; dry seasons, barren times, or 'in the wilderness' – a reference to Moses and the Exodus or Jesus' forty-day fast in the desert. Christians who should know better sometimes call it 'backsliding' and refer to the prodigal son, as though these silent times are somehow our fault. We are then back to the folly of trying to repent of some secret sin.

What on earth happened to this life of grace? You told me it didn't depend on me and my performance. Jesus takes me as I am and accepts me unconditionally. Suddenly, now that I've signed up, you seem to have changed the rules. It's all down to me after all. But I did the right things. I didn't reject him, but he seems to have rejected me! What the fu— oops, sorry, I tried to improve my language, too! – what on earth is going on?

This is precisely where dualistic thinking lets us down. He loves me; he loves me not. If it's really like that then we can never know where we are, and we might as well cut our losses and give up now. Who wants a God who changes with the wind?

God is not fickle; everything we read of people's devotional experience in the Bible suggests that although there may be good times and bad times, God remains totally committed to us. So what is actually happening?

My answer, applying helical theology, is just this: nothing unusual. It's what we should expect. Just as we experience cycles in everything else in life, so it is with spiritual life. It may seem uncomfortable but it is nothing to panic over and certainly not a reason to give up. Remember our life, death, resurrection pattern; recall that this forms a single triangle of grace and love. All that is happening is that you are going through a 'death', or a 'humility' part of the cycle, without which there could be no triangle of grace in the first place. The way into grace also sets the pattern for the way forward. It may seem rough and at first confusing but there is no way that you have fallen from grace, no way you have lost God's love, no way that he has or could ever truly abandon you. Although it may sound contradictory, the very fact that you are experiencing one of these silent times is evidence that you are spiritually alive and in the purposes of God. If you were dead you would have no feeling.

Sounds daft? No more so than trees bare of leaves in winter. Look closely during these 'death' times and you will see spring buds beginning to form that will burst into new life as the winter passes. Trees are not dead in winter; they just look that way.

Likewise, for many married couples a woman's period is not the best time for lovemaking and many couples give it a miss for a few days. Does the fact that they are not enjoying the ecstasy of intercourse mean they have ceased to love one another, that the marriage has died? Of course not! For many people that temporary absence serves to build up desire so that they come together again with renewed passion – a process that reinforces just how much they do love and desire each other. A monthly resurrection, no less!

Remember this is how the universe is, because that is how God is, and it could be no other way. Your silent time is simply part of the rhythm of life.

25. Growing Up

There must be few parents who don't at some point cry out to their children, 'Why don't you grow up?' On our beach you will mostly find children playing happily, but then one of them will start a squabble over a bucket and spade. That may then lead to stamping on a brother or sister's sandcastle, and the ensuing tantrums. Thus the parental intervention, 'Grow up!'

Naturally, we don't mean this physically. Children have very little control over that side of their development. Usually, the cry is in response to some childish behaviour, sibling squabbles, an attack of the sulks, or a tantrum because they can't have their own way. Parental exasperation is justified if the child in question should know better by now. The fact that many don't may be due to a variety of factors, not least of which is the emphasis on rights without responsibility so prevalent in our contemporary society. Well, I would say that as a parent and a grandparent, wouldn't I? Conveniently overlooking my own youthful follies, of course!

So, what do we mean by growing up? Physically, we most want our children to be healthy and to avoid injury, but as emerging adults we look for something more. We would like them to do the best they can with their lives and achieve personal happiness. It's our hope that they will find good friends and know how to get on with people. We expect that our love for them will mature to the point where they will love us in return as adults.

If we are good parents, we will wish that they find out what life is for, a purpose, a faith, a sense of direction. These are far more important qualities than the acquisition of academic qualifications, cars, spouse, children, home of their own, and job with prospects. These are all legitimate pursuits but they are not the point of life. Unfortunately, many people don't understand this until much later, and some sadly never get it at all.

When God created Adam and Eve as innocent, inexperienced children in understanding, he allowed the Fall (as well as allowing for the Fall), with the clear intention that we should grow up. In fact, that we should grow into something better than Adam and Eve. They might have loved God as children love their parents, but the goal is that we should love God as full-grown adults. That does not happen automatically, even less so in a society obsessed with staying young and where spiritual development isn't even on the curriculum.

This is the way of love. Parents love their children as babies, enjoy teaching them all about life, even take pleasure in their blossoming adolescence. At every stage we experience a loving relationship with our children, but the real goal is lifelong adult friendship, that free choice on their part to love us as we have always loved them.

God has nothing less in mind.

Training and Testing

Of course, parenthood and parental love is not a smooth upward path. Life is full of undulations; we have to ride the waves of events and emotional responses to events. Growth takes place through a series of mini deaths and resurrections, not by isolating and insulating them from reality. The overly sterile world of the disinfectant advertisers is bad for our children's health because they develop adult resistance to disease by exposure to grubby surfaces as children. We inoculate them against the real killers by injecting them with greatly weakened toxins so that they will produce antibodies.

Likewise, love is tested when children are naughty. We don't kill our children or maim them in punishment; yet the rebuke, the denial of privilege, the requirement to say sorry, is an essential part of the process in producing a socially well-adapted adult rather than an overgrown pig!

Failing an exam or two teaches children that they can't take their studies for granted. Essential learning if you want to hold down a job in today's competitive market. The hard graft of apprenticeship, of private practice, the frustration of trying to get it right, produces the craftsperson or the musician. No pain, no art.

When I trained as a gym instructor, our ex-marines coach would have us hanging from the wall bars with our legs at right angles for minutes on end. His favourite expression while we struggled to hold the position was, 'It's the one that hurts that does you good!' Every decent athlete will tell you that it's true. Training is paining. Our Olympians who command worldwide fame for their extraordinary achievements must first undergo months and years of arduous training, endless setbacks and personal defeats, until they are of the calibre to be among the best. Even more to be admired are our para-Olympians who overcome astonishing adversity, but arguably would have remained unknown were it not for their disabilities and the opportunity to turn their sufferings into glory.

Training involves pain and discomfort, sacrifice and cost. If we are to grow up as people, to attain wisdom, to fulfil a life of love, to have a genuinely satisfying inner life that expresses itself in love for God and for our fellow beings, then it will follow the now familiar helical process. Growth, that is, replacing our existing state with a resurrected life that is better, is only possible as we pass through the death phase.

Let me give you a couple of illustrations of what I mean. The first serious book I wrote was totally shredded by an author that I respected and had requested to critique my work. I left his home shell-shocked, disappointed and devastated at the revelation of my own incompetence. I would bin the manuscript and never write again! In fact, I kept it and tried to learn from this humbling experience. Slowly but surely, I learned my craft and that led in time to the success of my first published book, *Hagbane's Doom*. Like they say, and many books later, the rest is history. The point of this is that if you don't somehow embrace the death, there can be no resurrection, no future. You remain stuck in your immature state.

My mother lost part of her leg below the knee when she was eighteen years of age. With typical understatement she said she cried when she came round and saw the result of the operation. She came from humble origins and grew up in poverty. Who wants to employ, let alone marry, a poor uneducated cripple? Well, she took on the challenge of adversity, created an alphabet from car number plates, taught herself to read and write. She found work, and found Christian faith. In time, she found an RAF man, and produced three boys, living long enough to see her grandchildren and great grandchildren. I don't know how she did it but I admire her immensely for turning adversity into a life worth living. The last time I saw her before she died she was chuckling to herself. I like to think she was already seeing what it would be like in heaven to have two whole legs again!

We cannot grow up to be the people God wants us to be without passing through this process, and repeatedly so. Some of it will come about because we choose to embrace the training; some will be very much against our will, adversities that come our way unbidden and unwelcome. We may not choose our circumstances but we do choose how we respond to those circumstances. Once we see that the crises in our lives are an invitation rather than a judgement, an opportunity to grow, then we can make some sense of them.

Suffering shifts our boundaries and perceptions. It offers us a different life from the one we planned. For some the physical limitations will enable us to concentrate on the growth of our souls. For others, the emotional traumas will lead us into caring professions, or relocate us and, as we undertake the journey, introduce us to new relationships. My son, who nearly died in an horrific motorcycle accident, married the nurse who sat with him above and beyond the call of duty when her shifts ended.

One thing is certain: suffering confronts us with a choice to grow or not to grow. This is why blaming God for all that is wrong is not only illogical but futile. All the time we do that our lives stagnate and ultimately that stagnation creates our own hell. For in my understanding hell is simply life leading to death with no resurrection – and that is our choice or otherwise.

The Story of Job

Let's take a further look at the experience of Job. This ancient story addresses the age-old problem of why good people sometimes suffer misfortune. The historical references set it around the time of Abraham, c.1800 BC, in a place called Uz, possibly in Syria or Saudi Arabia.

The dramatic tension of the book centres on a wager between God and Satan. The bet is simple. Job's devotion to God is surely dependent on his successful earthly life. Take that away and Job will prove to be just another time server who believes in God because it's easy to do so. Without being told why, Job is then tested by the devil with God's permission. As a result, he suffers multiple tragedies that test his faith.

The deeper question is whether goodness or evil is the ultimate reality, and that turns on Job's response.

This question confronts us repeatedly. Think of the First World War trenches, the Nazi concentration camps, the Soviet gulags, the killing fields of Cambodia, the Bosnian genocide, Syria. Many lost faith and hope during these human atrocities, but there were those who, like Job, hoped against hope and believed that goodness would triumph in the end even if they did not survive to see it. They were right; the devil lost the bet. When Job's wife says, 'Curse God and die!'(Job 2:9), he refuses. God is still good, all the time, in spite of apparent evidence to the contrary. There is no surrender to the triumph of evil.

Totally failing to understand what is going on, Job's well-meaning companions with eloquent poetry bring up an old chestnut. Surely Job has committed some secret sin. How else could this disaster have befallen him?

Job protests his ignorance concerning what is taking place in his life, but also his innocence. This isn't a proud boast but a matter of honesty. Whatever the answer to the question 'Why do the innocent suffer?', they are innocent! Those who have to find a guilt reason for suffering are simply dualistic linear thinkers. God must be good, so we must be bad, and our sufferings must be a punishment. Total twaddle!

Helical theology recognises the familiar pattern in Job's life. He may not have sinned but that didn't mean he had reached maturity. The devil was right; Job had it easy. He was a protected child who had never faced adversity even though he was an adult in years. As a wealthy man he automatically commanded respect, and he could afford to be kind to the poor without any serious personal cost. Left to himself he would have continued in spiritual infancy, worshipping a local 'bless me' cultural deity for the rest of his days. Something had to give if he was to grow up.

It has been well observed that the Tester (God), tests us so that we might pass; the Tempter (Satan), tests us so that we might fail. Both are at work in this story, but God will most certainly have the upper hand.

Job had grown complacent and had fixed the limits of God according to his experience of God's goodness. If he is to grow up then he must follow the life, death, resurrection cycle. His moral uprightness will be challenged; he will be humbled as people draw back from him, fearing contamination. His logical conclusion that he is innocent in spite of what others may say, is not enough. Indeed, his self-justification could just as easily become infantile pride. In truth, Job had reduced God to a matter of logic within the limits of his puny experience.

One of the concerns I had in writing this book is that I might fall into the same trap. My antidote is the same as that which God prescribed to Job. He took him to task by asking Job how much he really knew of cosmic structures, of physics, astronomy, chemistry, biology, and wildlife. Like Job, I must conclude that I am pretty well ignorant of almost everything. I am but a man constrained by the limits of my existence. God, on the other hand, is boundless, limitless, eternal. The more I understand about the size and complexity of the universe the more I realise that God is greater and more unfathomable. I cannot master the subject; I can only worship with awe and gratitude.

Job's humble response released the mercy of his resurrection. He prayed for his annoying friends and his sufferings passed. God blessed him even more and he lived to a ripe old age. Job had grown up.

How God Grew Up

It's all very well arguing that God puts us through – or rather allows us to go through – hard times so that we can grow up, even though there is the risk that we might refuse and fall into a self-made hell. But what about him? Are we still dealing with some kind of impassive Greek god who has neither idea nor interest in what it feels like to hurt as a human being – with the small proviso that it is all for our own good rather than simply divine caprice? Is God a cold-hearted being, too tough for us? Is he relentlessly putting us through the mill to achieve some divine goal of his own?

Those poets with deeper spiritual experience of God than me write words like:

As a father has compassion on his children, so the Lord has compassion on those who fear him; for he knows how we are formed, he remembers that we are dust. (Psalm 103:13–14)

Such a God is not ruthless; he is kind, and understanding. Fair enough, but surely a good leader is one who only asks people to do what he himself has done. How can God show true compassion if he has never experienced pain?

Or has he?

The greatest demonstration of God's compassion and empathy with our condition is found in Jesus of Nazareth. The Christian claim is simple: God came to live with us, to experience first-hand what it is like to be human. He didn't come to a palace or a place of privilege like some other religious leaders. He arrived in a struggling community oppressed by a totalitarian invader, watched over by religious thought police, in a working-class environment, surrounded by poverty and disease.

If that were not enough, he was barbarically tortured to death as a common criminal. Denied all human rights, cursed by his community and abandoned by his followers, rumour has it that even God dumped him – the ultimate self-rejection.

This act of humility by God smashes for ever the Deist idea that God is somehow distant and indifferent to us. It gives the lie to the impersonal clockwork universe that can allow for no divine intervention. They called Jesus Emmanuel, which means 'God among us'. He has lived our life, and died our death – and he knows what it feels like.

We may at this point accuse God of cheating. It is easy for Superman because he knows he can always get out of trouble, so long as you keep him off the Kryptonite! Surely Jesus was the same; God is in disguise but able to zap anyone who causes trouble; he can pelt his opponents with angelic firebombs with a flick of his fingers. Isn't that what his miracles are about? Surely then, much as we might welcome Emmanuel to our planet, if only for a little while, he is anything but like us, really.

We think like this because we have not grasped just how radical the humility of God is. Controversially, he joins himself to the ovum of a young teenage peasant girl, allowing his opponents to suspect that he is a bastard and his mother a slut. He is born in poverty and raised in obscurity. His parents are for a while refugees. He learns a builder's trade but his father dies young leaving him responsible to provide for his mother and his younger siblings. His embracing of humanity means he has to learn just like the rest of us, as a child, as a teenager, as a man. Even the Son of God had to grow up (Hebrews 5:8–9).

It is not until he is baptised at the age of thirty, and the Holy Spirit empowers him, that we see hints of who he really is. All his miracles are done as a man like us but are possible because of his humble cooperation with the Spirit of God, and his determination to do only his Father's will.

Even so, he does not go to university and become a great academic; he never makes it with the upper classes or with wealthy tradespeople; there is no trophy wife; he does not raise an army and fight for a political or religious cause; he never becomes a guru in a temple or a mystic holy man. In secular terms he is a poor God, and at the end of his life he is a wounded God – despised, rejected, mutilated and abandoned. In Jesus, God experiences the reality of what it means to face death and to die.

Now, if you have been following the argument of this book, the subsequent resurrection of Jesus should hardly come as a surprise. It fits the pattern perfectly; he has made the journey from the life of heaven to the depths of human suffering. It was not theoretical for him; he walked the talk, felt the pain, underwent the suffering, and through it all kept his faith and trust in God, even to his last breath. In so doing he becomes the first of a new breed of humanity: Resurrection Man! He is the final stage of human evolution; someone who has defeated death, attained supra-physical powers and lives for ever without corruption in a renewed universe that one day will be accessible to all who want it.

In the truest and fullest sense, by losing his life Jesus found it immeasurably more so. He had grown up. He discovered and pioneered for us the truth that 'in all things God works for the good of those who love him, who have been called according to his purpose' (Romans 8:28). With God nothing is wasted. So writes the apostle Paul whose own experience led him to say,

For I am convinced that neither death nor life, neither angels nor demons, neither the present nor the future, nor any powers, neither height nor depth, nor anything else in all creation, will be able to separate us from the love of God that is in Christ Jesus our Lord. (Romans 8:38–39)

When and how that works out for the rest of us is the subject of the last chapter. Meanwhile, we must explore a little more what worries us about growing up.

26. Fearing to Grow Up

When I was young I wished I was older; now I am older I wish I were young. Or do I? It's fun to recall our youthful pranks and exploits, but who would really want to be a teenager all over again? Eternal youth holds little attraction for those who have truly grown-up. Yet our society is afraid of maturity and even despises it.

Old people, we hear, are a threat to the economy; we can't afford to pay their pensions. This is, of course, complete nonsense; the elderly not only make a phenomenal contribution to society through their voluntary activities, their childminding and engagement in community projects, but most of them are still taxpayers and they spend their money, providing employment for vast numbers of younger people. Yet, in spite of the grey economy being worth billions to the nation in reinvested pension spending, our media continue to churn out the same old nonsense that suggests older people should consider themselves a burden on society.

Then we have the obsession with trying to look like Barbie dolls. Why Botox away your life story? Why cover your face in a mixture of chalk, grease and plastic polymers so that you look as false as a shop window mannequin? Make-up is one thing, a complete daily re-plastering job is another! Of course we should look after ourselves and make the best of what we've got. That is simply a matter of self-respect, but the quest for eternal youth suggests a deeper problem in our society.

All the while we are treating maturity as a threat, as something to be masked, we are missing the importance of inner growth.

We are failing to appreciate the value of wisdom and experience. Growing up is not the same as growing old; indeed, to grow up is in a sense to grow young. Perhaps that is why those older people who say that they are young in heart are not altogether wrong.

There is another sense in which our society fears growing up. It is in the multiplication of laws, of petty rules and regulations, of endless bureaucracy, of checklist diagnosis and treatment, of health and safety over common sense. All this serves to keep people immature. It takes away the responsibility to think for ourselves, to learn wisdom and apply it to life. This is hardly surprising in a society that focuses on linear dualistic thinking, on simple yes-no answers to complex issues that actually require a different way of thinking. 'I kept the rules, I followed the correct procedure,' appears to be more important than, 'I did the right thing morally and spiritually.'

Rather than creating the freedom of adulthood we have imposed a new Pharisee-ism on ourselves. Instead of trusting people, we control them. Let me explain what I mean. When Jesus walked the earth his society was heavily regulated by a ruling class called Pharisees. These people went far beyond the Ten Commandments, creating hundreds of petty laws to regulate behaviour. It produced an external conformity but did nothing to enable personal growth. In fact, Jesus exposed the hypocrisy of the lawmakers themselves like a good investigative journalist might today. Instead of freeing people, the laws kept them in reins like toddlers in the street. What lay behind this nanny state mentality was a fear of letting people grow up and take responsibility for their own lives.

Spiritual maturity came to be defined as sin management; that is, expertise in keeping all the rules. This elitist mentality quite wrongly carried over into Christendom. So we define a saint as somebody who never breaks the rules, the ultimate goody-goody, the holier than thou. One thing is for certain, we cannot and we do not want to be like them! They become the icons of the unattainable, and usually with skin that no amount of Botox is going to fix!

I want to relieve you of a worry. Growing up has nothing to do with sin management. You do not have to take up an ascetic life of fasting, celibacy and self-flagellation. You do not need to embark on a process of endless heart-searching, raking over every little sin and fault that you can recall in your colourful life, you do not have to attend confession, sacred or secular, to receive absolution for all your petty misdemeanours. Growing up, reaching maturity, does not mean seeing how uncomfortable you can make your life. In fact, many things should become much easier. Maturity is less about holiness, purity, perfection than about attaining wisdom, love and grace. It's not sin management but grace appropriation that we should aim for. Then the sins more or less take care of themselves.

Jesus radically challenged this religious mentality, to such an extent that his opponents considered him an anarchist. In actuality, he made it quite clear that he did not come to abolish the law, but to give it its full and proper meaning in terms of a heart relationship with God. The entire dualistic approach to life where goodness equalled blessing and sin equalled cursing, the 'weighted scales of justice' model, is over. Jesus threw the scales away! From now on we will do life differently, and make all the silly little rules redundant.

As with the case of Job, Jesus' way would be a mighty gamble but it would produce spiritual maturity, that is, people filled with love for God and for their fellow humans, and wisdom for living that they could pass on for the good of society. This is what the apostle Paul meant when he described the law as a peripatetic school teacher whose job was to lead people to Christ rather than to produce experts in rules and regulations.

The goal is not sinless perfection, which is a futile and unattainable end in this life, and a contradiction of the mucky reality of human existence. Instead, it is to grow up into a profound personal relationship with God.

The apostle John uses the simple metaphor of a child becoming a teenager and in time a parent to help us grasp this process (1 John 2:12–14). It is a great bit of helical theology in which John identifies three stages of spiritual life. The first is that of the child who knows two things: they have a personal relationship with God, the source of their spiritual life; and they are accepted without any guilt or condemnation.

The second stage is that of the young person, the spiritual teenager. This is the age of proving, of testing, of fighting and winning the battles of life. It corresponds to the 'death' part of the cycle, the difficult challenges. During this process the young person learns to fight and defeat the playground bully, the roaring lion, the Tempter, the evil one. The truth, the word of God, is no longer an external guide and corrective. It becomes embedded in the heart; it becomes our word as well as God's. The outcome is an adult who is spiritually robust.

The final stage in this life is that of the mature parent. What characterises them is not the list of their attainments and acquisitions but their relationship with God. In fact, it is their second naivety, their return to the simple trust and security of a child. The big difference, however, is that they have made the journey, gone the full cycle, garnered the experience. They have lived out life, death and resurrection. They have grown up.

The Naughty Corner

There is something terribly immature about evil, about wickedness. Ultimately, the criminal mind is childish and nowhere is this more apparent than in our law courts when arrogant and sophisticated criminal minds are revealed to be no more than those of little kids. You know the sort of thing: I want to do it my way. I'm the king of the castle. Everybody's got to do what I say. I want your toys for myself. Just like the kindergarten! It wasn't me, it was him. If you don't do what I want I'm going to tell on you! If you show me your bum I'll give you one of my sweets. I'm going to get my own back.

I'll beat you up after school. Me and my mates will say you did it. My dad's bigger than your dad.

Judges must be driven spare by having to listen to this drivel all day!

Now I am not minimising evil or writing like some wishy-washy liberal who wants to lay the responsibility for criminal actions on some indefinable entity like society; justice has to be done and people have to take responsibility for their actions and pay the price. Children must learn that they cannot have it all their own way, and it is better they are taught that by means of good parenting when they are young in years and the stakes are lower, rather than waiting until they are adult and the consequences of crime and punishment are that much more severe.

My real point is that we cannot hope to grow up unless we deal with the issue of wrongdoing in our own lives.

I have left this until now, not as a sting in the tail but because some churches put so much emphasis on what they call sin that it distorts the entire Christian message, and I at least do not want you getting the wrong idea. A non-Christian woman once told me that she found work as a teacher in a Christian school. With no knowledge of faith she asked them what it meant to believe. She was told, 'You are a sinner and if you don't repent you will go to hell!' She said to me plaintively, 'How could they say that? They don't even know me!' I agreed with her and apologised for the stupidity and insensitivity of those who apparently profess the same faith as I do.

That said, only an arrogant, self-righteous and dishonest person will claim that there is nothing wrong with their behaviour or their thought life. That really is childish!

The real question is this: does our wrongdoing present us with an impassable barrier to having anything to do with God and growing up? Well, from our side apparently, yes. People say things like, 'I could never be good enough.' 'I've done too much wrong in my life.' 'There's too much to give up.' On the other hand we have those who declare, 'I'm as good as the next man. Are you accusing me or something?'

The first disqualify themselves by surrendering to the power of their existing experience; the second by their unwillingness to humble themselves. In both cases the path to growth is blocked.

What about from God's side? However much he might love us can he really ignore the fact that he is just? What would be the use of a God who in the end let everybody off and told them to be nice from now on? We are constantly frustrated and outraged by people who get away with their evils. Is there no justice in the universe? The Greeks believed that hubris would be followed by nemesis, pride comes before a fall, but that just is not true in so many instances.

If God does exercise his justice in some eternal manner, where does he draw the line? Do only the really bad guys get it in the neck? If there is a line then how can I be sure I am on the right side of it? This, you will recognise, is the problem of linear bipolar thinking.

So how does helical tripolar theology address the problem?

Very simply, it takes the issue of the line of relative good and evil, or of justice and mercy, and throws it into the field of grace formed by the three poles of justice, mercy and humility.

Grace is God's rescue package. It is his way of solving his problems and ours.

Amazing Grace

We use the word grace to describe beauty; in that sense a thing may be mathematically and artistically elegant, beautifully proportioned and harmonious, like the finest things of life. It also conveys the wow factor, like a performer totally in harmony with their gifting producing a spectacular achievement that leaves us stunned and ecstatic all at once, and even more so if it was unexpected. We get the word 'charismatic' from the Greek word for grace and underneath it is the bestowal of a gift. God's grace is elegant and stunning, and it is a total gift.

It all focuses on the reason Jesus died. This was all about God being just, merciful and humble all at once by taking our place and applying his own laws to himself. He became the representative wrongdoer for all of us and took the rap in all humility. The path of bearing our evil became the route whereby evil is transformed. Still acting as one of us, he showed mercy to himself and rose from the dead. Brilliantly, he then invites all and anyone who wishes to align themselves with Jesus to enjoy the same benefit without any cost to themselves. It's as though he let himself contract the killer disease so that we might obtain immunity by receiving his antibodies into our own bloodstreams. Benefitting from this free inoculation is as simple as saying goodbye to our old life and receiving new life through an act of faith in which we associate ourselves with Jesus.

Is this fair? Of course not! Since when was love fair? Is it fair that a loving parent should sacrifice their life to save their child? Is it just that a soldier might die to save his comrades? Is it fair that someone should willingly give their life to protect their sworn enemy? No, it's grace. Incredible, outrageous, amazing, beautiful grace!

This is the cosmic good news at the heart of the Christian faith. Everyone who feels inadequate, guilty, unclean, unworthy, lost, confused and oppressed is welcome to come. All those who are fed up with the hypocrisy of self-righteousness and want some reality are welcome to benefit. All the rebels against God are invited to lay down their arms before a God who has disarmed himself to win us back. That includes all atheists, agnostics, persecutors, pagans, Christians, Muslims, Hindus, Buddhists – members of any religion or none.

On offer is peace with God, the forgiveness of all our wrongdoing, the gift of God's good Spirit, new purposeful life, inner moral strength, an enlightened mind, an ability to love and to be loved, hope for the future, and the release of genuine spiritual growth with the expectation of heaven to follow, and one day the resurrection of our own mortal bodies. What not to like?

27. Releasing the Flow

I feel passionately about justice and I am an instinctive supporter of the underdog. If I am honest, there are times when I wish the bastards dead who persecute the weak and the innocent. I hate violence and especially so when it is directed against women and children. All torturers should rot in hell, along with rapists, drug barons, warmongers, murderers, thieves, child abusers . . . (By the way, child abusers are not paedophiles. That misnomer means lovers of children. These people hate children. It's not about love or even sex; it's about power and coercion.) I'll stop there, because in the end I will find myself throwing everyone into hell, including myself!

Helical theology is about reconciliation and mercy, resurrection and transformation – and that must involve forgiveness. Many ills that we face are the results of other people's stupidity or malice. My friends and family and I have experienced both and it's especially not easy to forgive those malicious people who stick the knife in. There are plenty of non-murderous psychopaths out there!

Now let's have some clarity about this matter of forgiveness. To forgive does not mean minimising evil, nor is it about absolving people from guilt. Criminals should not be excused facing trial and punishment because we choose to forgive them. When Jesus spoke about loving your enemies it was in the context of our personal response to evil. He never released the state from its God-given responsibility to exercise justice. Forgiveness is not wishy-washy, 'there, there, they couldn't help themselves', nonsense. The swines who hurt you are still swines even though you may choose to forgive them, and they will still face the judgement of God even if they escape human justice. But human justice there should be, nonetheless.

Your humble, self-dying act of forgiveness will not likely change them, but it will change you. It will enable you to come through your sufferings and to grow stronger. The alternative is to live with an inner bitterness and an endless desire for revenge that will either be frustrated or, if you are successful, will make you just like your enemies. This is why the Christian version of the just war theory calls nations to exercise proper justice but not vengeance. Behave like your enemy and you become the enemy. You will have lost the war.

Without forgiveness and reconciliation at the personal level, the future can only be one of endless familial, tribal, religious and cultural vendettas. So, in Paul's words,

Do not repay anyone evil for evil. Be careful to do what is right in the eyes of everyone. If it is possible, as far as it depends on you, live at peace with everyone. Do not take revenge, my dear friends, but leave room for God's wrath, for it is written: 'It is mine to avenge; I will repay,' says the Lord. On the contrary: 'If your enemy is hungry, feed him; if he is thirsty, give him something to drink. In doing this, you will heap burning coals on his head.' Do not be overcome by evil, but overcome evil with good. (Romans 12:17–21)

The one stanza of the Lord's Prayer that Jesus commented on was, 'Forgive us our sins as we forgive those who sin against us.' His telling comment was this:

For if you forgive other people when they sin against you, your heavenly Father will also forgive you. But if you do not forgive others their sins, your Father will not forgive your sins. (Matthew 6:14–15)

Nuff said!

Forgiving often has to be an act of the will for a long time before it becomes an act of the heart, but it is worth persevering with, like a long-term medicine. One day you wake up and realise that the pain has gone. You can live again.

Miracles

You may well be reading this book because you could do with a miracle, either for yourself or for someone else. The outmoded street theology of Deism by definition excludes the possibility of divine intervention and, therefore, of miracles. Despite all the evidence to the contrary they can't happen.

However, helical theology most certainly does allow for miracles and I'm pleased to report that they happen today and in all countries of the world, not only in the realm of healing but in all kinds of other divine and angelic interventions. It would be very tempting for me at this moment to reel off a whole list, or to provide a pile of case studies, but that is not the point of this book. Ask around and you will find all sorts of people with amazing stories. Like the virtually blind lady with two cataracts who kept falling over and whose heart condition made surgery difficult. Someone prayed for her in one of our meetings and instantly her cataracts disappeared and she could see clearly. Or the wheelchair-bound MS sufferer who was found leaping and dancing in the back hall because God had touched her body. Or the man dying of stomach cancer who was, after prayer, completely healed and went on to live to a ripe old age.

So, leaving aside the nutty 'aliens turned my granny into a goldfish' press, why don't we read about these in our newspapers? Why was a recent miraculous restoration of sight witnessed by many at a holiday camp not on the ten o'clock news? I can only conclude that the news writers are cynics too prejudiced by their own bigotry to acknowledge what is taking place. We don't even waste our time reporting these things to the media any longer.

Meanwhile, ironically, 'science correspondents' will regale us with wonders, discoveries, cures and proofs based on evidence so flimsy that no serious scientist would give it a moment's credence. And this, complete with 'real' pictures that are totally computer generated. Computers count, ultimately that's all they do; it's people like you and me that tell them what to count. Computers project; they do not prove. For all our advances in technology the basic rule still applies: trash in, trash out. So don't buy into the lie that they can only report what is proven to be true beyond doubt and so have to exclude reports of miracles, when even in the realm of science they resort to speculation. Incidentally, I never quote a miracle unless I know it is medically attested to.

OK, I've had my little opinionated rant about the bias of our media when it comes to miracles! Back to the plot.

That miracles happen in answer to prayer is beyond reasonable doubt. Having said that, and however welcome they might be to somebody in need of one, we should not overrate their importance. Miracles played a significant part in the ministry of Jesus but even he expressed caution because his mission was not primarily that of a miracle worker. He came to reveal God and call people to faith so that they might grow to be the people they were meant to be.

Miracles in his ministry were signposts to faith; they were not 'proofs' of the 'show us a miracle and we will believe' kind. His response was, in effect, 'No, you won't; you will be impressed but that will not necessarily lead you to faith. You might even be angered, because the miracle may be performed on someone you really don't like, or you don't think deserves it, or in an unapproved manner, or even on the wrong day of the week!' Just imagine for one moment that a paedophile was healed of deafness at a meeting in a prison and the news got out, while your very decent self-sacrificing sister did not get healed at a similar meeting in the local community hall. Miracles can be controversial.

We must add to this, in our day, the confusion over what constitutes a miracle. The old Victorian view, expressed by the philosopher David Hume, that miracles must be a suspension of the laws of nature, and by definition inexplicable, is still around.

Now, scientifically there may be an element of truth in this if we propose a parallel universe, for there might be powers in that universe that we cannot imagine because they operate on a different molecular basis. We might suppose that some of those powers could temporarily enter our universe. After all, the writer of the Bible book called Hebrews talks about the powers of the age to come – if you like, another universe – having already begun to fall on us.

Personally, I am more comfortable with the idea that a miracle or a healing is simply a better use of the existing powers of this universe. For example, it is possible to walk on liquid custard, because it is a non-Newtonian fluid (don't worry what that means, but you can see it in one of the repeats of *Brainiac* or on YouTube). So what is to stop Jesus walking on water since he would understand physics better than any of us? Why should he not speed up healing processes that might need fifty years so that they took only fifty seconds? We can do reconstructive surgery, why not him, except that he didn't need a scalpel and needle and thread.

Whatever the explanation, the real issue is, can I expect a miracle, a remarkable healing in my life or that of my child? Here I can give you no certain answer. I have seen a good deal of genuine and remarkable healing in answer to prayer and healing touch. I have also seen some genuine and remarkable non-healing using the same methods. There is no guarantee, and Jesus seldom used the same method twice, anyway.

The evidence suggests that the genuine is more likely to happen among the poor in the emerging world whose needs are vastly greater than ours, but that if you take a trip to the African bush, it probably won't work for you. The Spirit of God at times acts regionally and seasonally but don't go catching planes to the latest sensation destination, because you are likely to be disqualified by exceeding the baggage limit!

The best advice I can give you is to be open for a healing miracle but don't chase it. Faith was always present when Jesus healed, but faith is not working yourself up into a spiritual lather. It is not fasting for days, giving all you money away, discarding your tablets or insulin, repenting of everything you've ever done wrong, and helping old ladies across the road whether they like it or not! Faith is simple trust. A baby has faith when it is put to the breast; it sucks in faith and is hopefully rewarded, but even that isn't guaranteed.

More advice: never pay money either in fees or in a pressured expectation of you doing so, or in retiring offerings. The world is full of charlatans, con artists, religious as well as secular, who prey on the vulnerable. They will tell you they hear voices, their clever questions will make you think it's Aunt Maud from beyond, they will give you a show, push you over, punch you in the stomach, claim that you have received your healing and are as good as new even though you still have all the symptoms! They'll have you shake, rattle and roll. Use your common sense. However desperate you are, you are not so desperate as to throw away your brains. Jesus did none of this nonsense. Blessing does not depend on your geographic alignment, or on whether you holler or whisper your prayers.

There is no technique, no form of words, no special person with extraordinary gifts that can guarantee your healing. That doesn't mean there is no value in symbols and ritual. Our secular world revels in rituals, from coronations to military commissions, from marches to Mardi Gras, from festivals to funerals. Humans love dressing up in uniforms and performing familiar patterns. Symbols and rituals give order and stability to what otherwise appears chaotic. In the context of healing they may help us focus our distraught thoughts, but no ritual can of itself heal you. The most it can do is raise your expectation, as with those who touch relics or make religious pilgrimages to Lourdes or the Ganges. But if you are healed you could never say for sure whether that might not have happened just as easily in your front room.

As with any other sphere in life, the genuine can stand up to investigation. A healing miracle is not a feeling, it is a physical reality. If you think you have been healed then check it out with the doctor and don't go throwing away your crutches and medicines until it is verified. Now I have come across doctors who have lied because they can't cope with the fact that someone has experienced a miracle, but I have also known where doctors have written the word miracle on the hospital records, or at least, to be politically correct, 'spontaneous remission', meaning that the patient recovered by themselves without medical intervention or known reason.

One thing is certain, if you have been prayed for by a genuine person, irrespective of their ecclesiastical or other status, you will know that you are loved, and that God loves you. That is the key. Healing is not the exercise of power; it is the expression of love. If you are brought closer to God then you will feel a whole lot better. If you become fully and even miraculously healed as well then I am delighted for you.

Deliver Us From Evil

I met a woman some time ago whose leg had been severed by a train. She confided in me that as she lay on the rails there she could smell evil, a smell quite unlike anything she had ever experienced. I have met others with similar stories. Some speak of a malevolent force coming for them in the night, of the inability to breathe, and of the power in saying the name of Jesus, even though they are not necessarily religious people.

It is not my place to assess how subjective these experiences are but at the root of them lies fear and especially the fear of death. This the Bible certainly describes as satanic; in a brilliant example of helical theology the writer to Jewish Christians says of Jesus,

Since the children have flesh and blood, he too shared in their humanity so that by his death he might break the power of him who holds the power of death – that is, the devil – and free

201

those who all their lives were held in slavery by their fear of death. (Hebrews 2:14–15)

A lot of people respond by saying they are not afraid of dying – unlike those scaredy-pants Christian wimps again! It's missing the point; fear of death is about fear of loss, about losing control, being overwhelmed especially by evil. Fear of death motivates the bonehead with his pit bull terrier just as much as the mother fearing to lose her children or the man clinging to his job at any cost. Ultimately, we are back to the story of Job. Will evil prove to be the greater reality? Is the world ultimately insane?

The apostle Paul wrote these words to his fearful deputy, 'For God has not given us a spirit of fear, but of power and of love and of a sound mind' (2 Timothy 1:7 NKJV). Great words when you feel you are losing control, going mad, or just plain frightened.

Sometimes you need to call the bluff on your fear of death. Instead of fighting, just surrender. Invite it. 'Come on then, if that's what you want to do!' You will find you pass through the spectre, and the fear will abate. You will learn that goodness triumphs over evil. Another little resurrection of your own!

Other times it's good to fight back another way. You may be tempted to swear and curse when you are in great pain and spiritual anguish; you may just want to cry out in agony. There's nothing that the satanic playground bully likes better! So, try this: instead of the negative response, say 'Hallelujah', or 'Praise the Lord', or sing a good song, instead. That should wind the devil up a bit! Maybe he'll give up on you as a hopeless case.

Choosing to praise and give thanks in adversity is choosing to affirm the goodness of God and of his creation. Paul and his fellow traveller Silas were illegally flogged half to death and imprisoned at Philippi. Around midnight they started singing and praying. In their case it provoked an earthquake and their subsequent release from gaol. It might not do that for you but there are prisons made of invisible bars that still need smashing; strongholds of the mind and spirit that must be broken. Try a bit of divine music therapy and start a spiritual earthquake!

Helping Others

I suffered from regular guts ache when I was a kid and I recall an occasion when I was lying on the snow and ice doubled up in pain against a wall in the school playground. The pain was bad but the worst feeling was of rejection; nobody bothered, nobody cared, nobody came. Many years later I was healed of that experience when in a flashback vision Jesus came to me and took my hand, raised me up and said, 'Come on, John, let's walk together.'

Loneliness, isolation, rejection – the worst pains show no visible wounds.

All intelligent commentators on what is known as Jesus' cry of dereliction on the cross are agreed that this was the most profound mystery and agony of the whole terrible episode. '*Eloi, Eloi, lama sabachthani*?. . . My God, my God, why have you forsaken me?'(Mark 15:34 NKJV). God tearing himself apart to bring us together; God aghast at the corruption he bore for us so that we might be clean; God undergoing cosmic alienation so that he might reconcile, heal and mend the entire creation.

Having been through it, he is able to help us in our isolation. Indeed, God suffers with us; he empathises with our pain, shares again our death so that we might also experience resurrection. We never suffer alone. Jesus said, 'I will not leave you as orphans. I will come to you' (John 14:18).

The incarnation of the Christ, the coming to earth of Jesus, is the central pivot of history on which all else turns. When he ascended and sent his Holy Spirit into the world, he began to incarnate himself in the lives of his true followers, those who embraced the life, death, resurrection pattern. This means that we become the channels of his help and care for others, but now spread all across the globe.

Having received his help we are equipped to help others in their sufferings. Paul puts it thus:

Praise be to the God and Father of our Lord Jesus Christ, the Father of compassion and the God of all comfort, who comforts us in all our troubles, so that we can comfort those in any trouble with the comfort we ourselves receive from God. (2 Corinthians 1:3–4)

Part of the journey, a resurrection part, is to support others in their afflictions. Much of the time it just means being there, listening, occasionally offering a word of advice, easing the boredom of pain with something better than daytime TV. Sometimes you will be the presence of God as the Holy Spirit fills you with love and compassion borne of bitter experience.

As a traveller following the helical path you may identify yourself with the Franciscan Prayer:

Lord, make me an instrument of your peace,
Where there is hatred, let me sow love;
Where there is injury, pardon;
Where there is doubt, faith;
Where there is despair, hope;
Where there is darkness, light;
Where there is sadness, joy.
O Divine Master,
grant that I may not so much seek to be consoled, as to console;
to be understood, as to understand;
to be loved, as to love.
For it is in giving that we receive.
It is in pardoning that we are pardoned,
and it is in dying that we are born to Eternal Life. Amen.

This is the true purpose of the church; anything else is fiddling around while Rome burns. Our sufferings have purpose. We need not be rendered useless. The story that our lives have to tell makes us living parables of grace. The sufferings of Christ have become ours as we experience what it means to be part of the redemptive process that ultimately will transform the universe.

Therefore we do not lose heart. Though outwardly we are wasting away, yet inwardly we are being renewed day by day. For our light and momentary troubles are achieving for us an eternal glory that far outweighs them all. So we fix our eyes not on what is seen, but on what is unseen, since what is seen is temporary, but what is unseen is eternal. (2 Corinthians 4:16–18)

It is time to look at where our journey is taking us.

28. Human Destiny

J.R.R .Tolkien described the road as going on for ever, and in a real sense it does. This contemplative, reflective, relation-building journey has no end. There is no qualifying day, no winning post, no degree ceremony, no retirement. There lies before us, instead, the prospect of deeper discoveries, higher heights and broader vistas that grow throughout this life and take an exponential leap when mortality transmutes into immortality. We might call this timeless time; time no longer measured in linear or clock terms, but in quality. *Kairos* instead of *chronos*. C.S. Lewis, in *The Last Battle*, described the process as 'further up and further in'.[15] The great Story, the Adventure of God, goes on for ever.

However, our seashore journey must soon end and in this chapter I want to explore a few thoughts about human destiny. In other words, what is it all about? What is the meaning of life? Where is it all going? Is it going anywhere at all? To use theological language, this is the teleological or eschatological question. It is both personal and universal.

Our journey has suggested the reasonable idea that there exists a living God who creates and sustains the universe. The Alpha point, the beginning of time, occurred when Trinity God – the God of loving relationship, Father, Son and Holy Spirit engaging in an eternal helical dance, span out a three-dimensional dance floor that we call the universe. Time was born, and space. This dance floor exists in the creative tension of justice, mercy and humility, filling the cosmos with grace and love.

Focusing on our planet, God created people in his image to share in the sacred dance. But love required that he give us absolute freedom of choice in the matter. Human history demonstrates unmistakably that we chose to do our own thing. Three-dimensional relationship was replaced by two-dimensional materialism. We became egocentric, combative, destructive, greedy to find security in things. We began to worship creation instead of the Creator. This is 'the sin of the world' from which all other evils flow.

That did not stop God loving us and he instituted a process that would bring this prodigal world back to himself, ever seeking to sweep us up into the dance through acts of grace and kindness. The dance touched earth most especially when God revealed himself in Jesus, emptying himself sufficiently to experience the fate of us frail humans. The scenario into which he came combined the most sophisticated example of religion, with the politics of the most dictatorial military empire, and the culture of the greatest intellectuals of the day. It was the best we could come up with not having a living relationship with God. All subsequent history is but footnotes on those critical times.

They crucified him, of course. Such divine love fitted the conventions of neither religion, politics nor academia.

Yet that death and subsequent resurrection brought to fruition a radical process of restoring humanity to its original glory and better. Jesus did not come to condemn the world but to rescue it. From insignificant beginnings the stream of love and grace has proved unstoppable, just as we might expect. God will not fail in his purpose and the end of the story is not a hell packed with sinners but heaven celebrated by an innumerable company of people from all nations, cultures and classes.

The death leads inevitably to resurrection on a cosmic scale. As Paul expressed it:

For God was pleased to have all his fullness dwell in him [Christ], and through him to reconcile to himself all things, whether things on earth or things in heaven, by making peace through his blood, shed on the cross. (Colossians 1:19–20)

The Alpha point will surely reach its Omega point.

The Way is Upward

I occasionally describe myself as a Christian humanist. How is that possible? Surely a Christian believes in God, and a humanist believes in man? I don't find it a problem. My faith in God leads me to believe in man, and my faith in man leads me to believe in God. I believe in the ascent of man because I believe in the ascent of Jesus.

The physical ascension of Christ may seem naive in our sophisticated days of space travel but his dematerialisation still beats anything we can do, and it does for all generations convey the completion of the growing-up story of his life. He enters the parallel world dimension that we commonly call heaven, and he does so as our pioneer, assuring us of our own heavenly destiny.

There's a fair taking place on the beach. It includes a helter-skelter. Helical theology offers a kind of reverse helter-skelter. Instead of spiralling downwards out of control, or more likely just plummeting to our doom, energised by the Holy Spirit, we find ourselves rising upwards through the spiralling phases of life and death, light and darkness, growing lighter and more alive all the time. The apostle Paul wrote, 'Therefore we do not lose heart. Though outwardly we are wasting away, yet inwardly we are being renewed day by day' (2 Corinthians 4:16).

This is not a fragile hope based upon our individual performance. Paul uses the phrase *en christos*, in Christ, 164 times. It refers to the here and now security of being intimately in relationship with God through the connecting point which is the eternal Christ, the second Person of the Trinity. This is the same Christ who was revealed on earth for a brief but history-changing time in Jesus.

So, we are 'in Christ' and Christ is in us. Paul calls this the hope, or certainty, of everlasting spiritual life, i.e. heaven.

Applying this principle to human history, in spite of all the ups and downs, human progress has continued and all the indications are that it is going somewhere. If there was an Alpha point then conceivably there can be an Omega point, a beginning and an end. From an evolutionary perspective, if you accept the mechanism of natural selection then evolution points upwards. Natural selection is helical; a species appears, fails adequately to adapt when under pressure and disappears to make way for something better. This is the theory of the dinosaurs being replaced by mammals and culminating in ourselves.

There is no reason to suppose that God has not willed this. At no point throughout this book have I questioned that God is in charge. Of course he is! What I have been asking is *how* he is in charge. We have discovered the helical pattern of life, death and resurrection and paralleled it with justice, humility and mercy. On the basis that what God requires of us must be true of himself, we have deduced that Trinity God is just, humble and merciful and that's how he runs the world.

Learning to recognise the pattern and make the right response to it is the key to living, particularly during times of adversity. It is what we mean, or should mean, by living in the will of God, or finding our true selves in relationship to him.

As I have indicated, my journey into faith began many years ago and it did so because of a fundamental curiosity. I wanted to know the meaning of life. So I began exploring. Religion in the formal sense held no great attraction for me; I never attended Sunday school or a church service as a child. Since science and art interested me in equal measure, my approach to faith was phenomenological, pragmatic. Did it work? Did it make sense? Did it inspire? Did I find some reasonable examples? Was it sufficiently global? Did it give me enough grounds to deal with my unexplained weird or liminal experiences? Did it offer me a credible cosmology and a teleology – a future?

On this latter point I found churches quite confused and confusing. The last book of the Bible, the Revelation of John, or the Apocalypse, made real and compelling sense to me when I first read it. I could see the pictures in my mind's eye, get the message, experience the drama, understand what was going on. It played a significant part in my journey into faith. However, when I spoke to Christians they all told me it was a very difficult book and hard to understand. I was puzzled.

Then I learned that there were interpretation packages that were imposed on the text and all of these differed. I came across words like dispensationalism, rapture, post-millennialism, pre-millennialism, a-millennialism, naff jokes about pan-millennialism 'because it will all pan out in the end'! Then there were the gloating sadistic stories that delighted in the Christians disappearing while the world was left to rot; and unbelievable time charts about when all this was to take place, weeks that had no length, complex codes, and 'the mark of the beast' being just about anybody we didn't like!

This stuff still goes on and to my mind it is entirely missing the point, which is simply that God is completing the helix, bringing the Fall to an end and renewing the cosmos to be even better than the original creation because it will be inhabited by people who have evolved into those who love God with the childlike freedom of mature adults. People who have made the journey.

Faith favours progress. It is not static or passive. Despite its popularity I have never liked John Lennon's 'Imagine' for the simple reason that if it were true he could never have written the song! Life requires creative energy, ups and downs, conflict even. Drop out too much and you drop dead, with or without an assassin's bullet.

The apostle Paul describes creation in rhythmic terms – note the helical pattern – of being in labour to achieve our final destiny. He writes,

That's why I don't think there's any comparison between the present hard times and the coming good times. The created world itself can hardly wait for what's coming next. Everything in creation is being more or less held back. God reins it in until both creation and all the creatures are ready and can be released at the same moment into the glorious times ahead. Meanwhile, the joyful anticipation deepens. All around us we observe a pregnant creation. The difficult times of pain throughout the world are simply birth pangs. But it's not only around us; it's within us. The Spirit of God is arousing us within. We're also feeling the birth pangs. These sterile and barren bodies of ours are yearning for full deliverance. That is why waiting does not diminish us, any more than waiting diminishes a pregnant mother. We are enlarged in the waiting. We, of course, don't see what is enlarging us. But the longer we wait, the larger we become, and the more joyful our expectancy. (Romans 8:18–25 MSG).

A day is coming when life will cease to be subject to entropy; futility and death will be no more. Even the Fall is not ultimately futile; it is simply following the pattern of life, death and resurrection. So, our present struggles are infused with hope. They are part of the birth process that will bring about the defeat of death and the transformation of the entire cosmos. The Alpha point may require us to run through the entire language of life, but there will come an Omega point that will herald a new heaven and a new earth.

That this will happen is underwritten by the historic physical resurrection of Christ. He is the forerunner of a future that we can all be part of, if we will – and we can experience the spiritual aspect of this right now in our present situations.

29. A Happy End

Our journey, or at least this part of our journey, ends with a wedding on the beach. The bridegroom and his supporters, his family and friends are assembled before us. All eyes are on a winding stair that descends from a cliff top lost in radiant mist. The stairway is lined on both sides with bridesmaids clad in shimmering gowns of brilliant rainbow hues. This is a big wedding! We pause, our eyes drawn to the glorious figure slowly emerging from the mist, descending the steps with stately grace and humble dignity. Her dress is stunning and she is beautiful beyond words. Our mouths drop open in awe. We watch as she reaches the sand and her bridegroom makes towards her. He has eyes for no other, and she none but for him. Love is in the air. It is tangible and we find ourselves bathed in its aura. Instinctively we know that this love is the one to which all our lesser loves have been drawing us throughout our lives. Yet we are not excluded; we are invited to the party. Eager hands wave us forward into this buoyant, luminous air. We are coming home.

To my mind there has been too much sensationalist talk about the end of the world, about Armageddon, and the supposed order of final events – and far too much heat expended on the subject by those who should know better. What are they trying to do, frighten us into loving God? Duh! What matters is that the culmination of history, of creation itself, is filled with hope for everyone. God has no plans to scrub out everything he has made, including us, so that he can start again and maybe get it right second, or is it third, fourth, fifth, time round! Those who critique my scribbles and dribbles may be quite right to suggest that I should start again, but this does not apply to God!

The goal isn't the destruction of the universe, or Armageddon, though that may be part of the story. It is the bride of Christ coming down out of heaven, the healing of all things, the abolition of evil, the consummation of love and the renewal of the cosmos.

God loves us and he has no more desire to annihilate those made in his image – those he has fathered – than we sane humans wish to kill our own children. In a real sense we create our own destinies by our choices and behaviour. This is why, in the context of the ancient Israelites, God said, 'Do you really want to die because of your sins? I, the Lord God, have no wish for that to happen to anyone. So change your ways and live!' (Ezekiel 18:31–32 author's translation).

It is not God's desire that anyone should perish. He would much rather we got our act together and aimed for glory, rather than wallowing in a self-destructive obsession with our own egos. As Jesus said, 'What will you gain, if you own the whole world but destroy yourself?' (Matthew 16:26).

God's plan and desire, the goal of creation, is to produce people who freely love him and one another. These are people who lose their first life in order to find new life. In other words they pass through the helical process by willing choice, even transmuting their sufferings into glory.

That this should apply to just a tiny minority is to my mind bordering on blasphemy. One of the great appeals of the Christian faith is its universality. By this I do not mean that God will take pity on us without any action on our part. That would represent a failure of his purpose. We need to engage with the process.

What I mean is that the genius of Christ was to teach and live a faith that had its roots in Abraham's stepping out on a journey of faith that would extend to the whole world. At the Council of Jerusalem in AD 50, some 17 years after Jesus' death and resurrection, the early church leaders finally got it; they realised that salvation was by faith and by grace and nothing else.

Race didn't count, so everyone could apply without a DNA or cultural test. Education and social standing didn't count, so sages, senators and slaves were equally welcome. Gender was of no importance, so men and women had the same access and privileges. A new global unity in diversity became possible, and without the use of force or violence. We could all grow up and put away the squabbles of two-and-a-half-year-olds that characterise so much of our politics and social systems.

So, is no one excluded? Only those who want to be. Jesus invited everyone to turn up just as they were and without any spiritual or moral wash and brush up, including those with low self-esteem, those facing despair, the powerless, those with a passion for justice, the compassionate, the true-hearted, the peacemakers, the persecuted and the oppressed. No previous experience is required; you don't have to be born into it. Indeed, you can't, and to quote a cliché, the only way in is to be 'born again'! You are not too bad to apply; and you are not too good to apply. As Jesus said, 'Whoever comes to me I will never drive away' (John 6:37).

What about those who don't even believe in God? I respect intelligent atheists, just as I do people of other faiths; I hope you have the common decency to reciprocate that respect to us faith people. And God still loves you and still invites you! He is more interested in our hearts than our heads. What we think is often culturally conditioned, but in our psyches we may be crying out for the reality of a spiritual life. In which case we could begin to sample a new paradigm of living and explore a relationship with God even if, for a while, we continue to call ourselves atheists.

What about people of other religions? My simple answer is this: it's not the label on the door that counts but the label on the heart. We reap what we sow, under whatever label we do it. Although Jesus is the Way, the Truth, and the Life, and his message is one of sacrificial love and grace to all people, there are many of other religions who recognise spiritually what this means, and order their lives accordingly, even if they don't yet know his name. We judge outwardly, but God looks upon the heart.

I cannot believe for one moment that God went to all this trouble, outworking his vast eternal and glorious purpose, for the sake of some tiny remnant to inhabit an exclusive heavenly club. That would make him the loser. I work on the assumption that everyone is being drawn home unless they really don't want to be and they behave accordingly. So, let's not fear the future. Instead, let's join the sacred dance in the here and now. All of us!

A Taste for Heaven

I've always wondered what's so very wrong with 'pie in the sky when you die'. I quite like pie!

OK, I understand the reaction. An escapist faith that has no care for the suffering mass of humanity, a selfish insurance policy to heaven that ignores any engagement in the social, political and economic structures, is a faith to be despised. I believe that the church does have a prophetic role to play in society; it should speak out. I don't believe in the privatisation of religion; the church should be fully engaged in the community right now. In reality, this is true. We find God-lovers deeply committed to social care all round the world. The church is the biggest humanitarian organisation on the planet – just as it should be.

However, that is not the whole story. If the parallel world that we call heaven exists then it's reasonable to suppose that, freed from the constraints of mortality, people who have journeyed in search of knowing God should one day find him fully and without restriction. They should see the face of God and be overwhelmed with wonder. Like one of the dying thieves at Calvary, they should enter a state called paradise and be happy for ever. As the apostle John suggests, we are now already children of God. 'And that's only the beginning. Who knows how we'll end up! What we know is that when Christ is openly revealed, we'll see him – and in seeing him, become like him. All of us who look forward to his Coming

216

stay ready, with the glistening purity of Jesus' life as a model for our own' (1 John 3:2–3 MSG).

Would anyone really not want that, particularly for those who suffer? Why would the helix cease at physical death for someone who has already experienced an inner resurrection? While I fully understand that no one wants to suffer for ever in this life, and why we may legitimately talk about a blessed release for those in great pain, it doesn't follow that they should face annihilation rather than glory. In fact, given the choice I would rather pass away believing in the 'myth' of heaven than in the 'myth' of annihilation. The existence and therefore the accessibility of this parallel reality is assumed throughout the New Testament. It is based on the resurrection of Christ but also a variety of divine encounters and helical logic. The disciples meet up with the risen Christ in a number of well-attested encounters. The apostle Paul has his Damascus Road experience; angels are the agents of numerous supernatural interventions.

As for the helical logic:

The Spirit himself testifies with our spirit that we are God's children. Now if we are children, then we are heirs – heirs of God and co-heirs with Christ, if indeed we share in his sufferings in order that we may also share in his glory. I consider that our present sufferings are not worth comparing with the glory that will be revealed in us. (Romans 8:16–18)

So, let's not imagine the renewed creation as the cartoonists' depictions of floating cherubs and us drifting among them in nightshirts, sporting long white beards (ladies too?) and plucking harps. Instead, it is a cosmos in which perfect communication between God and ourselves is now a reality. What we call prayer or saying prayers is transformed into genuine purposeful conversation. We will at last have grown up. This is what lies behind Paul's great chapter on love so often quoted at marriages but often misunderstood at the end:

When I was a child, I talked like a child, I thought like a child, I reasoned like a child. When I became a man, I put the ways of childhood behind me. For now we see only a reflection as in a mirror; then we shall see face to face. Now I know in part; then I shall know fully, even as I am fully known. (1 Corinthians 13:11–12)

It will be the biggest and best party ever. Millions of angels, uncountable numbers of people, yet everyone feeling special and welcomed by God as much as if they were the only one present. All of us celebrating the brilliance of what Jesus has accomplished for us.

Heaven's fireworks! The splendour of God and angels rejoicing! I'm looking forward to having my pie and eating it!

Journey's Real Beginning

We set out on an exploratory journey, and death or even heaven might seem to mark its end. However, that is only the beginning. God will not leave the job half finished. His plan is to reconcile all things to himself and that will mean him renewing the entire cosmos.

Yes, the world as we know it will end but it will immediately be superseded by a renewed one. Evil will finally be destroyed, as will death and all that is associated with it. Call it a lake of fire, or outer darkness, or a black hole if you will. These are only metaphors for the end of all that is corrupt and corrupting in this world, but they represent the reality of what happens to all that rejects the love of God, that denies grace, that chooses not to surrender the ego and so has no resurrection. Hell is self-chosen; don't blame God for it.

As C.S. Lewis put it: 'There are only two kinds of people in the end: those who say to God, "Thy will be done," and those to whom God says, in the end, "Thy will be done." All that are in Hell, choose it. Without that self-choice there could be no Hell.'[16]

That said, the emphasis is on renewal and healing, on redemption and reconciliation. We do not need to fear the end of the world. God promises us a hope-filled future. This is why, for those of us who suffer, the end is described as 'a new heaven and a new earth' and the new home city pictured as heaven sent, like a bride beautifully dressed for her husband. And a voice proclaims: '"Look! God's dwelling-place is now among the people, and he will dwell with them. They will be his people, and God himself will be with them and be their God. 'He will wipe every tear from their eyes. There will be no more death' or mourning or crying or pain, for the old order of things has passed away." He who was seated on the throne said, "I am making everything new!"' (Revelation 21:1–5).

The story that began in a garden concludes with a garden city where stands, bridging the river of life, the tree of health and healing for all nations.

This is when finally we shall have all our 'why' questions fully answered. We will discover, as with Job, that we were more important than we thought in the great conflict between good and evil. We shall know why our particular lives and experiences mattered, and why our right responses were so vital. Our sufferings will have counted; they never were random or futile.

Included in all this is the return of Christ in his eternal splendour, and the physical resurrection of those who love him. This is God being faithful to his own helical nature. Our bodies lived; they died; they must surely rise again. What happened to Jesus will happen to us. As to when, well, nobody knows, and anyone who claims to know is a charlatan or an idiot, so don't take a blind bit of notice of them. When it happens it will happen! Meanwhile, let's get on with living and loving.

All I will say about the resurrection of our bodies is that they will be the fulfilment of all the best sci-fi dreams. Our powers will be supra-physical, our strengths enhanced, our abilities unlimited by death or disease or human corruption. We shall create and explore a limitless universe where those virtues of beauty, truth and love will find their fullest and eternal expression in the contemplation of God in his infinite splendour. Not only that but we will have unrestricted opportunity to explore and to create in this marvellous new cosmos.

Sometimes when you walk along a sandy beach on a warm sunny day, the light ahead is a bright shimmering mist and the detail of what lies ahead isn't clear. That is the nature of the Mystery of God and his purposes. But, as with the beach, we walk on, drawn on into the shining, and as we do so what was hidden in the haze becomes ever clearer.

At the beginning of this book I invited you on a journey. My modest part as your guide is over, but the journey isn't. I hope you will keep travelling on, and I wish you well until the completion of your life's pilgrimage – to the day when the bright mist of the future gives way to the full heavenly glory of the Mystery himself, and life unlimited. I look forward to seeing you there.

Meanwhile,

May the road rise up to meet you.
May the wind be always at your back.
May the sun shine warm upon your face;
the rains fall soft upon your fields and, until we meet again,
may God hold you in the palm of his hand.

Endnotes

1. Quoted by Jonathan Langley in the April 2016 issue of *Premier Christianity.*

2. Julian Barnes, *Nothing to Be Frightened Of* (Vintage, 2009).

3. Arthur Koestler, *The Ghost in the Machine* (Hutchinson Publishing Group Ltd, 1967).

4. John Keats, *Endymion* (1818).

5. Archbishop Rowan Williams. Quoted by kind permission.

6. Sir David Brewster, *Memoirs of the Life, Writings, and Discoveries of Sir Isaac Newton* (Volume II. Ch. 27), (originally published in 1855).

7. C.S. Lewis, *The Lion, the Witch, and the Wardrobe* (Reprint edition HarperCollins, 2009). Copyright © 1950 by C.S. Lewis Pte. Ltd.

8. Stephen Hawking, *A Brief History of Time* (Bantam Press, 1988).

9. John Milton, *Paradise Lost* Book 12.

10. Paul Billheimer, *Destined for the Throne* (Bethany House Publishers, 2005).

11. Alexander Solzhenitsyn, Nobel Lecture 1970.

12. Martin Luther King, *Strength to Love* (Hodder & Stoughton, 1964).

13. W.E. Henley, *Invictus* (1888).

14. C.S. Lewis, *Mere Christianity* (Signature Classic edition HarperCollins, 2016). Copyright © 1942, 1943, 1944 by C.S. Lewis Pte Ltd.

15. C.S. Lewis, *The Last Battle* (Reprinted edition HarperCollins, 2008). Copyright © 1956 by C.S. Lewis Pte Ltd.

16. C.S. Lewis, *The Great Divorce* (Signature Classic edition HarperCollins, 2015). Copyright © 1946, 1973 by C.S. Lewis Pte Ltd.